Frederic Dan Huntington

Helps to a Holy Lent

Frederic Dan Huntington

Helps to a Holy Lent

ISBN/EAN: 9783337284992

Printed in Europe, USA, Canada, Australia, Japan

Cover: Foto ©Lupo / pixelio.de

More available books at **www.hansebooks.com**

HELPS

TO

HOLY LENT.

BY THE
... OF CENTRAL NEW ...

E. P. D... Y,
CHU...

Entered, according to Act of Congress, in the year 1872, by
E. P. DUTTON & CO.,
In the Office of the Librarian of Congress, at Washington.

LANGE, LITTLE & HILLMAN,
PRINTERS, ELECTROTYPERS AND STEREOTYPERS,
108 TO 114 WOOSTER STREET, N. Y.

INTRODUCTORY NOTE.

It has been thought by several friends that a little work like that which follows would be acceptable, and of some use. The plan is very simple, and will be recognized at a glance. For each of the days, from Ash-Wednesday to Easter Even, a few thoughts are offered, such as might not otherwise come to mind, to assist the spiritual exercises of this sacred season, both by giving a special theme and perhaps increased freshness to private devotion, and by connecting the closet with ordinary life.

To those who are familiar with the principles and history of Church-worship it will hardly be necessary to say that each daily portion, including something of Holy Scripture, meditation, hymn, and prayer, bears an analogy to our liturgical appointments, and is a kind of faint reflection in miniature of the order of Divine Service.

In order to meet as many personal tastes and shades of sentiment as possible, variety has been consulted as respects style and subjects, due regard being had to truth of doctrine. A considerable part of the pages is original. Most of the Collects are taken from English sources, though many of them are traceable to a more Eastern origin. Among the names of foreign authors from whose writings extracts have been made are those of Vaughan and Newman, Liddon and Robertson, Pusey and Isaac Williams, Avrillon and Schauffler, Krummacher and Stopford Brooke, Goulburn and Faber, Ken and Keble, Bonar and Dora Greenwell.

The book has been prepared with interest. It is sent out without pretension, and with the hope that, being received into friendly hands, it may make some hearts stronger and some lives more like the life of our Lord.

F. D. H.

SYRACUSE,
Feast of the Conversion of St. Paul.

HELPS TO A HOLY LENT.

Ash-Wednesday.

Set your affection on things above, not on things on the earth. For ye are dead, and your life is hid with Christ in God.

That thou appear not unto men to fast, but unto thy Father which is in secret: and thy Father, which seeth in secret, shall reward thee openly.

To appoint unto them that mourn in Zion, to give unto them beauty for ashes, the oil of joy for mourning, the garment of praise for the spirit of heaviness; that they might be called trees of righteousness, the planting of the Lord, that He might be glorified.

WE are not to look on this appointment of a penitential season as an arrangement of our own. It is rather a sacred part of that divinely ordained system of spiritual ministries by which the Lord quickens the consciences and trains the holy life of His children. Traces of such a solemnity of forty days' continuance are found all along through the earlier and later ages of Revelation. We know that it was the discipline of prophets, the reverential school of saints who lived wonderfully near to God. Entering once more upon it we have not to contrive a scheme of self-improvement without the guidance of the Spirit and the Bride. He who hallowed Lent by the Great Fast on the threshold of His mediatorial work for sinful souls passes into this still retirement with us. All these coming days and nights He will be our witness and our companion. The sincerity or formality of our special observances will be known to Him. Our self-denials He will share. The vows we make will be recorded in His book of remembrance. As the Gospel for last Sunday told us, " Jesus of Nazareth passeth by." The cry of our blindness and our weakness will not need to travel far to reach His ear, nor will He ever rebuke it, either for its ignorance or its importunity. It is with Him we are to walk all the way going up to Jerusalem.

There is one kind of suffering which we are not simply to accept and bear; we are to ordain the pain for ourselves, to go after it, to pray that it may be made keener than it is. This is penitence. If we do not know what that sorrow is, we are so much farther from true peace. It is because we have been living only on the surface of life, unmindful of its deeper realities, not seeing its grander glories. Both Christ and His forerunner, when they began to preach the Gospel of the Kingdom to the world, uttered one sharp, piercing call: "Repent!" They did not always go into minute specifications of every shade of sin, for they knew that they had for a witness a conscience in every breast, each heart knowing its own plague. They knew that there is always one comprehensive iniquity lodged farther in and spreading wider than any particular offence,—the sin of separation from God. In order to hate that the more heartily we must see it as it is, think about it, study its nature and workings, disentangle its sophistries and delusions, and appreciate the wretched comfort it gives to the adversary. Ashes must be sprinkled first before the ugliness in us can be changed to spiritual beauty. How significant the image is! Ashes are what is left when the fire is burnt out. They are bitter; worse than tasteless. They are pale. They are the sign of humiliation. No garment of praise can be put on till this spirit of heaviness has first wrapped its sackcloth about us.

Coming once more to the beginning of this gracious period we ought, first of all, to put away all superficial thoughts and all flippant conventional language about it. Do not trust to vague general intentions:—in the observance they will come to nothing, leaving only ashes in your mouth. Have a plan which you are not ashamed to own, and which you will probably be able to carry steadily through. So far as all arrangements of time and place and household are at your command, without wronging or disobliging others, make them yield to that plan. It is of less importance just what form your self-denial takes, than that it take some distinct form which you can define and present to your own mind. See that the Cross is really laid on somewhere. Nothing that you cut off from self-gratification for your Saviour's sake will you ever regret or wish to take back. Choose out, if you can, the weakest point. There is appetite in its several importunities; there is the passion for dress; there is idleness; there is the sin of evil speaking, in fact, all the foul brood of the transgressions of the tongue; there is bad temper; there is the lack of courage in manifesting your Christian convictions and bearing open witness;

there is the hurrying or forgetfulness of prayers; there is too little intercession; there is idolatry of the objects of human love; there is pride; there is the self-seeking or self-pleading that creeps even into your works of charity. Sprinkle the ashes where the moral deformity or disorder is most cunningly concealed, that the flesh of the inner man may come again like the flesh of a little child. Dismiss at once from the mind, and keep out of it, any notion that your sacrifices or repentances are to be reckoned to you as merits, or can furnish any ground for your justification. They are meant to bring your soul into that repentant, lowly, and teachable frame, where He who alone justifieth can set His healing and redeeming power more faithfully at work. They cleanse the vision; they open the door; they drive the tempter away, inviting in that heavenly Guest who stands now and knocks with patient solicitation, and who, once bidden by a sorrowing and self-renouncing faith to come in, abideth ever.

>Once more the solemn season calls
>A holy fast to keep;
>And now within the sacred walls
>Let priest and people weep.

> But not in tears and fast alone
> Let penitence appear;
> By holier life and love be shown
> That penitence sincere.

POUR into our hearts, O Lord, we beseech Thee, the grace of penitence, prayer, and lowliness, that, mortifying the flesh and living by the Spirit, and always meditating on heavenly things, we may think meanly of ourselves, and ever find our rest and glory in Thee alone, who livest and reignest with the Father and the Holy Ghost one God, world without end. *Amen.*

First Thursday.

Whoso dwelleth under the defence of the Most High, shall abide under the shadow of the Almighty. He shall defend thee under His wings, and thou shall be safe under His feathers. His faithfulness and truth shall be thy shield and buckler.

WE are entering upon that solemn season of the year when for a time we separate from each other as far as may be, and from the other blessings which God has given us. Like Moses, we have gone up into the mount to remain there forty days and forty nights in abstinence and prayer. We are called, as it were, out of sight; for though our worldly duties remain and must be done, and our bodily presence is in the world as it was, yet for a time we must be more or less cut off from the intercourse, the fellowship, the enjoyment, of each other, and be thrown upon the thought of ourselves and of our God. Earth must fade away from our eyes, and we must anticipate that great and solemn truth which we shall not fully understand until we stand before God in judgment; that to us there are but two beings in the whole world,—God and ourselves. The sympathy of others, the pleasant voice, the glad eye, the smiling countenance, the thrilling heart, which at present are our very life,—all will be away from us when Christ comes in judgment. Every one will have to think of himself. Every eye shall see *Him;* every heart will be full of *Him*. He will speak to every one; and every one will be rendering to Him his own account. By self-restraint, by abstinence, by prayer, by meditation, by recollection, we now anticipate in our measure that dreadful season. Let us not shrink from this necessary work; let us not suffer indolence or casual habits to get the better of us. Let us not yield to disgust or impatience; let us not fear as we enter the cloud. Let us recollect that it is *His* cloud which overshadows us. It is no earthly sorrow or pain, such as worketh death; but it is a bright cloud of godly sorrow, "working repentance to salvation not to be repented of."

> Forty days and forty nights
>   Thou wast fasting in the wild;
> Forty days and forty nights
>   Tempted, and yet undefiled.

FIRST THURSDAY.

Sunbeams scorching all the day;
Chilly drew-drops nightly shed;
Prowling beasts about Thy way;
Stones Thy pillow; earth Thy bed.
Shall not we Thy sorrows share,
And from earthly joys abstain,
Fasting still with instant prayer,
Glad with Thee to suffer pain?

O KING of heaven and earth, rich in mercy! behold we are poor and needy. Thou knowest how greatly we are in need, and thou alone art able to help and enrich us. O Lord, look graciously upon us, and from the treasures of Thy goodness succor the poverty of our souls, through Jesus Christ our Lord. *Amen.*

First Friday.

Ought not Christ to have suffered these things, and to enter into His glory?

We must through much tribulation enter into the kingdom of God.

I was like a lamb or an ox that is brought to the slaughter.

JEREMIAH speaks literally, in his own person as an individual, of the persecutions he endured; but, as a prophet, he speaks of Jesus Christ, who is that Lamb sacrificed in types, from the beginning of the world, in innocent Abel, and afterward in the Paschal Lamb, and in all the sacrifices of lambs which were commanded by the Law; but the real Lamb is the Lamb pointed out by John Baptist to his disciples, when he said: "Behold the Lamb of God, which taketh away the sin of the world."

Behold, then, this mild and patient Lamb about to be led to death because He so loved us as to take our sins on Himself that He might bear the punishment of them. That Lamb, who is God, is going to make on the Cross a wonderful union of two qualities, hitherto separate; that is to say, He will be both the priest and the victim. As a victim, He will pay our debts; as a priest, He will offer the one great and only sacrifice of our religion. The Cross will be the altar and the bloody cradle in which all the faithful will be born, and the firm foundation which will support the whole edifice of Christianity. Thence it comes that this Christianity has only been established in the world by sufferings, and it can only be established and supported in our souls by them; and it is for us, says St. Paul, to see how we shall build on this foundation by following the bleeding steps of the suffering Jesus. If you have ever seriously reflected on God's conduct toward you, you will see that, when you have strayed from the right path, it was by suffering that God brought you back again to the religion which prosperity had made you forget. In short, we then feel constrained to raise our eyes to heaven, we call upon the Lord; grace acts on our souls; we begin to feel that these sufferings were necessary to retrace in our hearts the almost effaced characters of the divine image. We see the extreme weakness of the creature, to whom we had recourse in the beginning of our troubles, and, convinced of the weakness of this resource, which at the most has only given us some fruitless consolation which did not free us from suffering, we turn to God, and, invoking Him with all our heart, we find in Him all that we desired, and we feel constrained to say, with the prophet: "Before I was afflicted, I went astray, but now have I kept Thy Word. It is good for me that I have been afflicted; that I might learn Thy statutes."

> Our faith would lay its hand
>   On that dear head of Thine.
> O Lamb of God, we stand
>   And there confess our sin.
> Oft look we back to see
>   The burdens Thou didst bear
> When hanging on the cruel Tree,
>   And trust our guilt was there.

O ALMIGHTY Lord, hear our prayers, grant our petitions in this time of grace and penitence; enable us to perform our religious duties with all the exactitude and reverence of which we are capable, and grant that the fasts consecrated by the example and precepts of Thy adorable Son may be pleasing in Thy sight, and may we finally obtain glory everlasting. And this we beg through the merits and mediation of Jesus Christ Thy Son our Lord. *Amen.*

First Saturday.

Ye are a chosen generation, a royal priesthood, an holy nation, a peculiar people; that ye should show forth the praises of Him who hath called you out of darkness into His marvellous light.

OF the whole Christian year, let me say that to live in it, and by it, is the best way of serving the Lord. Keep these days. If you cannot leave off your work on all of them, never mind, so you hallow them at least in your heart. O children of the Church! live in the Church, love her holy ways, walk in her paths of peace, look not beyond. You have naught to do with those who are without, but to treat them kindly, do good to them, and pray for them. In the Holy Catholic Church you have your portion; be content; give God thanks; be at rest. Live by the Bible and the Prayer Book. Begin each day with prayer; go forth to your work and to your labor until the evening; lie down with the eye of Jesus looking upon you, and the holy angels watching around. Do good in your time. Be sober, industrious, true, honest, kind. Fulfil your course. Lay hold on all the helps which the Lord puts within your reach to bring you to heaven. So shall your walk be close with God; so shall you at length rest in Him with the blessing of the Holy Church upon your grave; so shall you wake in the last great morning, to rise and go to your Father's House; to be brought close to that Lord of whose body you are a member, and from whose side you will never be parted; to inherit the kingdom prepared for you from the beginning of the world.

  Thus everywhere we find our suffering God,
    And where He trod
  May set our steps: the Cross on Calvary
    Uplifted high
  Beams on the martyr host, a beacon light
    In open fight.

  To the still wrestlings of the lonely heart
    He doth impart
  The virtue of His midnight agony
    When none was nigh,
  Save God and one good angel, to assuage
    The tempter's rage.

JESUS, our Master, do Thou meet us while we walk in the way, and long to reach the Heavenly Country, so that, following Thy light, we may keep the way of righteousness, and never wander away into the horrible darkness of this world's night, while Thou, who art the Way, the Truth, and the Life, art shining within us. *Amen.*

First Sunday.

The Lord send thee help from the Sanctuary and strengthen thee out of Sion.

And He said unto them, Come ye yourselves apart into a desert place and rest awhile, for there were many coming and going.

It brings our Lord in His humanity very near to us to find Him disturbed by the confusion of a crowd, and, while the weight of the whole spiritual creation rests perpetually on His heart, seeking rest from the world by an hour's retirement. There is at the same time a very beautiful disclosure of the tender thoughtfulness of His sympathy with His followers. His disciples have been busily toiling on His errands. He bids them come and learn something of His moments of rest. Come, He says, into this healing air of solitude. By a more intimate communion with Me alone gain a clearer comprehension of the great work of your life and of the peace which is its only reward, of the Cross you must daily bear, and the secret consciousness of Divine love which makes that Cross light. The Saviour appears to have been especially apt to go away alone at periods of peculiar difficulty, as if the girding up of His mind for the holiest acts of sacrifice could best be done apart from all mortal society. Having not where to lay His head He made the border of the desert His closet, or the mountain-top His sanctuary, watching unto prayer all night, wrestling for the world's salvation while the world slept, unmindful even of its need to be saved. In the spiritual history of men it is remarkable how often the commanding spirits that have done most to bless their fellows, and reform their age, have drawn their inward strength from above in such seasons of seclusion. Solitude is the Divinely appointed refuge of penitence, of self-examination, of holy resolutions yet new and feeble, of prayer. It is a means of grace; Christian character rarely obtains its heavenly flavor without it. When the Twelve withdrew from where many were coming and going, and did so *at His invitation*, they went deeper down than before into the realities of the Divine life, because, to speak as we do of our human intercourse, they had the Master all to themselves.

The expression, "Many were coming and going and there was no leisure," is strikingly descriptive of our times. We are hurrying on with a fast-living and outward-living generation, in a self-indulgent, showy, noisy age. The Church never needed the doctrine of religious stillness and retirement more than now. But the Church is made up of individuals, and I am among them. My loyalty to its honor, my independence of the tyranny of fashion, my cleanness from all the doubtful usages and social defilements by which I am tempted every day, my personal faithfulness to Christ, will be in proportion to the use I make of the seasons when I am apart with Him.

Many a dreary sunset, many a dreary dawn,
We had watched upon those desert hills as we pressed slowly on.
Yet sweet had been the silent dews which from God's presence fell,
And the still hours of resting, by palm-tree and by well,
Till we pitched our tent at last—the desert done—
Where we saw the hills of the Holy Land gleam in the sinking sun.

O LORD, may our souls perceive the sweetness of Thy presence. May they taste and see how gracious Thou art, that, filled with Thy love, they may seek nothing out of Thee wherein to rejoice ; for Thou, O Lord, art the joy of our heart, and our portion forever. *Amen.*

First Monday.

And Moses was there with the Lord forty days and forty nights. And it came to pass when he came down from Mount Sinai with the two tables of testimony in his hand, that Moses wist not that his face shone.

And as they came down from the mountain, he charged them that they should tell no man what things they had seen till the Son of Man were risen from the dead. And when He came to His disciples, He saw a great multitude about them, and the Scribes questioning with them; and straightway all the people when they beheld Him were greatly amazed, and running to Him, saluted Him.

Faith, if it hath not works, is dead, being alone.

If the way of faith and prayer runs from society to solitude, we must remember that the way of charitable work runs back from seclusion to society. In the perfect life of the Son of God this alternation is constant between seclusion and service, stillness and activity. We learn from it the law of our own religious growth. Precious as the periods of refreshment are, they are after all but temporary.

They are intervals of useful labor, not substitutes for it. Separation from men may possibly be sought for, owing to morbid moods, and it may create them. Like other means of grace, religious retirement has its peculiar temptations,—pride, unhealthy introspection, indolence, disparagement of other men. Accordingly, the real value of going apart into solitary places must be tested by the spirit with which we return from them into the ordinary engagements of our households and the world.

Lents, holy days, communions, special hours of unwonted elevation, must all be tried by that practical criterion. They are scattered along the Christian's road, Elims in his desert, banqueting-houses upon his march, to make the common time more sacred, the required work better done. The Church herself has to take her turn in lonely spots, sometimes in humiliation, persecution, and poverty; and it is in order that the Bride may be brought back to the Bridegroom more faithful in her love, more abundant in her sacrifice. "Therefore, behold, I will allure her and bring her into the wilderness and speak comfortably unto her. And I will give her her vineyards from thence, the Valley of Achor for a door of hope, and she shall sing there as in the days of her youth." Most of our time must be spent in the vineyards where we dig and prune. All rest is for the sake of that toil. The Sabbath is for man; the forty days are ordained to touch all days with a new sanctity. Our closets open from the places where men come and go. Something in our very prayers will be wrong unless we pass from them into the daily ministrations and drudgeries with more patience, more self-surrender, a kindlier forbearance with the infirmities of those around us, and a heartier effort to yield our interests to theirs for the Redeemer's sake. Our very rests will be unrefreshing without Him, and He only makes the retirement sacred, and society safe.

>Come, labor on:
>Who dares stand idle on the harvest plain,
>While all around him waves the golden grain,
>And every servant hears the Master say:
>>"Go work to-day?"
>
>Come, labor on:
>No time for rest, till glows the western sky
>While the long shadows o'er our pathway lie,
>And a glad sound comes with the setting sun:
>>"Servants, well done!"

FIRST MONDAY.

O LORD Jesus Christ, who hast declared that when we have done all that is commanded us, we are still unprofitable servants; give us grace so to fix our eyes on Thy most pure and holy life, that we may know our own impurity and sin, and seek in all humility to be conformed unto Thy will, Who livest and reignest with the Father and the Holy Ghost one God, world without end. *Amen.*

First Tuesday.

Be careful for nothing; but in everything by prayer and supplication with thanksgiving let your requests be made known unto God.

THERE is many a Christian who reaches nothing more than this (nay, who aims at nothing more), that devotion shall have its little hour in the day, and business its long hours; and great is his complacency if the business hours are not allowed to trench upon the hour of devotion. I am not saying anything against stated periods of devotion; they are absolutely essential, and it is only too certain that, in the absence of stated periods, the spirit of devotion would evaporate altogether. But I am saying that the soul will never taste a full satisfaction until it has learned more or less to mix devotion with work. The soul must not leave God for an instant if it is to be perfectly joyous and contented. Let it take but a step away from Him, and it is at once in a region of excitement and unrest, and so far forth, of danger. Remember that the New Testament teaching makes *unbroken* communion with God obligatory upon us. It names no seasons for prayer, or rather it names every season. "Pray without ceasing." My friend, I do not ask whether you have completely acquired the habit of interpenetrating your daily employments with the spirit of devotion (that is the case with none of us, least of all, probably, with the present writer); but are you placing this before you as your standard, and sincerely trying to reach it? Ejaculatory prayer is the great means of reaching it. Do you ever use ejaculatory prayer? Do you ever lift up your heart to God in the midst of your work, praying Him to shield you from temptation, to bless you in what you are doing, and, at all events, not to let you wander very far from His side? Do not say it is impossible; for to this and no lower standard you are called, both by the constitution of your nature and by the precept, "Pray without ceasing;" and, by the grace of God, all things which He commands are possible. You will say, perhaps, "I try to keep my mind continually in the right track; but, alas! it is thrown off its balance a thousand times a day by having to do things in a hurry and against time; by a warm conversation; by a piece of interesting news; by domestic worries and cares; by little rubs of the temper." So it is most truly. The mind wants steadying and setting right many times a day. It resembles a compass placed on a rickety table; the least stir of the table makes the needle swing around and point untrue. Let it settle, then, till it points aright. Be perfectly silent for a few moments, thinking of Jesus; there is an almost Divine force in silence. Drop the thing that worries, that excites, that interests, that thwarts you; let it fall like a sediment to the bottom, until the soul is no longer turbid; and say secretly: "Grant, I beseech Thee, merciful Lord, to Thy faithful servant pardon and peace; that I may be cleansed from all my sins, and serve Thee with a *quiet mind.*"

> The crowd of cares, the weightiest cross,
> Seem trifles less than light;
> Earth looks so little and so low,
> When faith shines full and bright.

O LORD of pity, who willest naught but good, leave me not to walk in mine own will; but overrule me to act at all times according to Thy will, which is always good. And have mercy on Thy creatures, and on me a great sinner; through Jesus Christ our Saviour. *Amen.*

Second Wednesday.

Let us humble ourselves therefore under the mighty hand of God, that He may exalt us in due time.

Without humility religious progress is impossible. Pride is the destruction of the principle of progress; it whispers to us continually that we are all that could be desired, or it points our attention to high positions and ambitious efforts beyond the scope of other men. Yet the true growth of the soul is not to be measured by our attempting many extraordinary duties, but by our power of doing simple duties well; and humility, when it reigns in the soul, carries this principle into practice. It bids us hallow our work, especially whatever may be to us hard or distasteful work, by doing it as a matter of principle. It bids us, when on our knees, use simple prayers. We do well to retain the very prayers which we used as children, however we may add to them; and to throw our whole soul into each separate clause and word. It enriches common acts of neighborly and social kindness with that intensity of moral effort which is due to every act of which the deepest moving power is the love of God. Without humility, no soul that has turned to God and is learning to serve Him is for a moment safe. The whole life of the living soul is the work of Divine grace; and while pride claims merit for self, and therefore goes before a fall, humility confesses, day by day, "By the grace of God I am what I am." The higher you climb the mountain side, the more fatal must be your fall, if you *do* fall: if you would look over the giddy precipice without risk, you must first stoop to lay firm hold on the rock of humility. For humility is the condition and guarantee of grace; and, as St. Augustine says, there is no reason, apart from the grace of God, why the highest saint should not be the worst of criminals.

> Thy breast to beat, thy clothes to rend,
>   God asketh not of Thee;
> Thy stubborn soul He bids thee bend
>   In true humility.

O let us then, with heartfelt grief,
　Draw nearer unto God,
And pray that He will grant relief,
　Will stay the lifted rod.

GRANT, we beseech Thee, O Lord, the true fruit of repentance to those who have wandered out of the way through sin, that they may obtain pardon for their offences, and be restored cleansed to Thy Holy Church; through Jesus Christ our Lord. *Amen*

Second Thursday.

Jesus answered and said unto her, O Woman, great is thy faith, be it unto thee even as thou wilt.

And this is the confidence that we have in Him, that, if we ask anything according to His will, He heareth us.

PRAY modestly as to the things of this life; earnestly for what may be helps to your salvation; intensely for salvation itself, that you may forever behold God, love God.

Cleanse your heart now: for "the pure in heart shall see God."

Be alone with God, that your soul may be free to speak to Him, and to hear Him. But be alone in your inmost hearts, shutting out busy, anxious thoughts, that they throng not in with the prayers, and cloud not the sight and thought of God.

Practise in life whatever thou prayest for, and God will give it thee more abundantly.

Bear patiently and humbly all daily crosses, contradictions, rebukes, and whatsoever is against thine own will. They will conform thee to the mind of God, be channels of grace which will cleanse thy soul for yet further grace.

Deny thyself things earthly, if thou wouldest taste the sweetness of things heavenly.

Above all things, persevere in prayer. Many begin well; many hold on for a time well; many pray well from time to time; some, alas! can even work themselves up from time to time to think they pray well, and to feel what they pray; many begin again and again well. Few persevere; for few they be who find the straight gate and narrow way which leadeth unto life.

If thou hast begun, pray that thou mayest pray better. If thou hast failed, pray to begin again, and to persevere. All who pray to persevere gain what they pray for. None who so prayed has perished.

> We need as much the Cross we bear,
>   As air we breathe, as light we see,—
> It draws us to Thy side in prayer,
>   It binds us to our strength in Thee.

O ALMIGHTY God, help Thou our weakness, and because we can neither perform nor even pray for what is right of ourselves as of ourselves, arouse by Thy Holy Spirit in our hearts groanings of prayer which cannot be uttered, that by Thy loving kindness there may be given unto us both the will to ask and the power to accomplish what is well pleasing unto Thee; through Jesus Christ our Lord. *Amen.*

Second Friday.

After that He poureth water into a bason, and began to wash the disciples' feet, and to wipe them with the towel wherewith He was girded. Then cometh He to Simon Peter: and Peter saith unto Him, Lord, dost Thou wash my feet? Jesus answered and said unto Him, What I do thou knowest not now; but thou shalt know hereafter. Peter saith unto Him, Thou shalt never wash my feet. Jesus answered him, If I wash thee not, thou hast no part with Me. Simon Peter saith unto Him, Lord, not my feet only, but also my hands and my head. Jesus saith to him, He that is washed needeth not save to wash his feet, but is *clean* every whit.

"Thou shalt never wash my feet," said the mistaken disciple. But listen to the Saviour's reply: "If I wash thee not, thou hast no part with Me." What an important declaration is this! You perceive how the more profound and mystic meaning of our Lord's act shines forth in these words,—namely, as having reference to the blood of atonement, to forgiveness, justification, and purification from sin. How much lies concealed in this passage, and how every syllable has its profound signification! "If *I* wash thee not." Yes, Thou, Lord Jesus, must do it; for who ever purified himself from sin? "If I do not *wash* thee." Yes, Thou must wash us; for teaching, instructing, and setting us an example is not sufficient. "If I wash *thee* not." Certainly, what does it avail me if Peter or Paul is cleansed, and I remain defiled? I must be forgiven, and feel that I am absolved; and it remains eternally true, that he who is not washed in the blood of Christ has no part with Him, nor in the blessings of His kingdom.

What is wont to happen in the progress of the life of faith? Unguarded moments occur, in which the man again sins in one way or other. He incautiously thinks, speaks, or does that which is improper, and is again guilty of unfaithfulness, although against his will; for only the devil and his seed sin wilfully: while he that is born of God, saith the Apostle, *cannot sin*. The man's walk is polluted; his feet, with which he comes in contact with the earth, are defiled. What is now to be done? First, beware of despondency, by which we only prepare a feast for Satan. Next, withdraw not from the presence of the Lord, as if his heart were closed against us. Thirdly, think not that it is necessary to make a fresh beginning of a religious life. The seed of the new birth remains within us; and the child of the family of God is not suddenly turned out of doors, like a servant or a stranger. "He that is washed," says our Lord, "is clean every whit: and ye are clean, but not all." Who does not now understand this speech? Its meaning is, He that is become a partaker of the blood of sprinkling, and of the baptism of the Spirit—that is, of the twofold grace of absolution from the guilt of sin and of regeneration to newness of life—is, as regards the inmost germ of his being, a thoroughly new man, who has eternally renounced sin, and whose inmost love, desire, and intention are directed to God and things Divine. Where such a one, from weakness, is overtaken by a fault, he has no need of an entirely new transformation, but only of a cleansing. He must let his feet be washed. Let this be duly considered by those who are in a state of grace, and let them resist the infernal accuser, lest he gain an advantage over them by his boundless accusations. Hold up the blood of the Lamb as a shield against him, and do not suffer your courage and confidence to be shaken.

When penitence has wept in vain
 Over some foul dark spot,
One only stream, a stream of blood,
 Can wash away the blot.

'Tis Jesus' blood that washes white,
 His Hand that brings relief,
His heart that's touched with all our joys,
 And feeleth for our grief.

O THOU who seest everything! I have sinned against Thee in thought, word, and deed. Blot out the handwriting of my trespasses, and write my name in the Book of Life. And have mercy on Thy creatures, and on me a great sinner; through Jesus Christ our Lord. *Amen.*

Second Saturday.

Ye see your calling.

Awake thou that sleepest, and arise from the dead, and Christ shall give thee light.

See then that ye walk circumspectly, not as fools but as wise, redeeming the time, because the days are evil.

ADDED time and added light make men worse unless they make them better. Old sinners are wickeder than young, and the world grows older. It is in the power of these last times, if they will, to sin more guiltily, and to scoff more blasphemously, than any earlier and less instructed century could. Each period, till the Lord comes again, demands a more circumspect obedience, and only sinks to a deeper disgrace if it is hollow in its professions or worldly in its life.

You say you have no responsibility for these vast streams of sin. Is that true? The weakest and youngest among us is answerable for a single life, to see that it is outwardly circumspect, and inwardly grafted into the life of the Son of God. These currents of evil are made up, every drop, of single lives. Let yours be right before God,— then your family, your acquaintances, all that you will have to answer for at the Judgment, will feel it, and be the better for it. That is what St. Paul means. That holy life of yours will go so far to redeem the time, and He who died to redeem both you and the world will accept you as one of His own.

We come, then, to the question, what ought the degree of a Christian's consecration to be in the world nowadays, and in a community like this where we live? How distinct ought the stamp of our Christian calling to be? How far ought the Christian man and the Christian woman and the Christian youth to be set apart, and stand alone?

There is but one answer, provided we seek the answer in the Word of God, where only we can find one in which we can safely rest. The form of the ordinary occupations of the holy man and the worldly man will not generally be very unlike, because the necessities of an outward livelihood are much the same, and it is not meant that, in this life, God's people and the world's should be outwardly separated; *that* separation is to come hereafter. But at this point their common life and their resemblance end. In the secret affections that prompt his spirit and govern his plans, his business, his amusements, his use of property and his tongue, the disciple of Christ is to show himself called by a distinct and peculiar calling. He is to stand so apart, in all these respects, that every observer of him is to take knowledge that he not only *has been* with Jesus, but that, there being two armies *always*, he belongs now to the one and not to the other. Every year, as the confirmation season comes round, one and another of those that are invited to make their confession of Christ before men excuse themselves. No excuse is so common as this : "I wish I were a true Christian ; I hope some time or other to be one, and a consistent one ; but I do not want to be another of those that I see too often, who say that they renounce this world for Christ, but alter nothing in their frivolity, or their passion for pleasure, dress, and gain, and with whom the only movement that distinguishes them from the most thoughtless is when they go, once a month, to take the Communion." Too great a work is on our hands, too solemn responsibilities are pressing, too great and glorious a Leader is looking at us and calling us, for this wretched trifling, which makes the Church look like the market and the ball-room, only ten times worse, for the inconsistency of its professions and the hollowness of its prayers. I say to you, as an English layman says: "If your life were but a fever-fit, the madness of a night, whose follies were all to be forgotten in the dawn, it might matter little how you fretted away the sickly hours; what toys you snatched at, or let fall; what visions you followed with the deceived eyes of your frenzy. Dance if you will on the floor of hospital wards; knit the straw into what crowns please you; gather the dust of it for treasure, clutching at the black motes in the air with your dying hands." But the delirium of thousands that live and die along these streets is a thousand times sadder than that, because the brain still keeps its accountability, and judgment is to come. Oh, you who bear the name of Christians, baptized and "chosen" to represent your Lord before men, gird up the loins of your mind. It will cost self-denial. It will bring on you the wonder, the criticism, the sarcasm, perhaps, of your social set. What then? For fifteen centuries Christendom has handed down with admiration the brave word of one of the Church's true priests, —" Athanasius against the world!" Why should we have to go back so far to find our saints, when there is the same opportunity, the same duty, for every disciple to stand against the social threat and flattery that are all the world to him? The girded loins, the sober mind, the unworldly walk— and the solitude of spirit if need be—shall we not cheerfully meet them, and resolutely take them up, for that glory that is to be revealed?

> 'Tis not for man to trifle: life is brief,
>   And sin is here:
> Our age is but the falling of a leaf,
>   A dropping tear.
> We have no time to sport the hours away:
> We must be working while 'tis called to-day.
>
> O day of time, how dark! O sky and earth,
>   How dull your hue!
> O day of Christ, how bright! O sky and earth
>   Made fair and new!
> Come, better Eden, with thy fresher green;
> Come, brighter Salem, gladden all the scene.

O GOD, who art of purer eyes than to behold iniquity, mercifully grant unto us such a sense of sin that we may receive cleansing, and such cleansing that we may be made pure in heart, and may see Thee for evermore; through our Saviour Jesus Christ. *Amen.*

Second Sunday.

Make me a clean heart, O God, and renew a right spirit within me.

Blessed are the pure in heart, for they shall see God.

In contending against sensual sins, the main stress must be laid on the principle of exclusion,—the absolute keeping away of bad suggestions and imagery from the mind. Once in, the stain has struck on a substance so sensitive that, if not quite indelible, it is still terribly tenacious and terribly prolific of sorrow. It is here, with beginnings, that we all have chiefly to do, in ourselves and our children. Here, peculiarly, the battle is secret and invisible. Not much can be *said*, and so the more must be done by prayer and instantaneous self-command, expelling the first contamination, and crying: "Cleanse Thou me from secret faults." In respect to many sins, self-examination may be safe and even necessary; but there are others where it is scarcely wholesome or profitable. Simple prevention, avoidance, the shutting of the eyes and ears, and pressing on to known duty, are the best security. It does not help much to go back and trace the ways of temptation. The wise man was right: "Avoid it; pass not by it; turn from it and pass away." "Lead us not into temptation." One wrong companionship in childhood, one unprincipled servant or schoolmate, one Mephistophiles using the advantages of superior station or intellect, may spread a curse through the whole hidden history of fourscore years. Next to bad companionship is a bad literature. The degeneracy of the public modesty, in the reading allowed without stint to the young, is a direct contradiction to both the profession and the fact of a progressive civilization. Books that are the products of a thoroughly unchristian social life, in both Europe and America, not only furnish the continual reading matter of the reckless and abandoned, but they stock the circulating libraries, and lie on the tables of the best-bred families, within reach of young persons from whose bodies and physical health every breath of outward malaria is warded off with incessant vigilance and at every cost. The harm falls just where the liability to harm is greatest,—on the springs of thought, imagination, emotion, where no direct effort can meet it or detect its inroads.

Best of all the protections against these impurities, however, after the prayer that entreats, in all the varying utterances of an intense devotion—"Create in me a clean heart, O God"—is incessant Christian occupation, with abstinence from those personal luxuries, idlenesses, and pamperings of the body, which are the preparations and provocatives of temptation. To turn swiftly and vigorously to some generous and righteous errand for the Master with a temperate and well-governed body, under a healthful regimen, and sometimes, perhaps, to make the body bear voluntary penalties for its errors, so as thereby to remind and regulate the soul, but at any rate to keep the thoughts and energies preoccupied, is the true mode of preserving Christian purity, and even of restoring it after it has been lost.

We must not fail to lift up our eyes toward the Seat of Mercy. "What are these which are arrayed in white robes? These are they which have washed their robes and made them white in the Blood of the Lamb. Therefore are they before the throne of God," serving Him face to face and heart to heart with the glorious angels that never sinned, seeing God. There is Love, Redemption, Forgiveness, and at last, the Beatific Vision, even for sinful hearts like ours.

A poet of few poems has written these verses, embodying the encouraging thought that, though the unfallen spirits excel in power and might, there is yet a singular blessedness belonging to those children of the Redemption who have known, after the wretchedness of impurity, the relief of repentance, and the rest of reconciliation:

> Earth has one joy unknown in heaven,—
> The new-born peace of sin forgiven.
> Tears of such pure and deep delight,
> Ye angels! never dimmed your sight!
>
> Ye saw, of old, on Chaos rise
> The beauteous pillars of the skies:
> Ye know where morn exulting springs
> And evening folds her drooping wings.
>
> Bright heralds of the Eternal Will,
> Abroad His errands ye fulfil,
> Or, throned in floods of beaming day
> Symphonious in His presence play;

While I amid your choirs shall shine,
And all your knowledge will be mine,
Ye on your harps must lean to hear
One secret chord that mine will bear.

CLEANSE us, O Lord, from our secret faults, and mercifully absolve us from our presumptuous sins, that we may receive Thy holy things with a pure mind; through Christ our Lord. *Amen.*

Second Monday.

I meditate on all Thy works; I muse on the work of Thy hands.

O how love I Thy law! it is my meditation all the day.

Mary kept all these things, and pondered them in her heart.

MEDITATION is partly passive, partly an active state. Whoever has pondered long over a plan which he is anxious to accomplish, without at first distinctly seeing the way, knows what meditation is. The subject presents itself in leisure moments spontaneously; but then all this sets the mind at work,—contriving, imagining, rejecting, modifying. He knows what it is who has ever earnestly and sincerely loved one living human being. The image of his friend rises unbidden by day and night; stands before his soul in the street and in the field; comes athwart his every thought, and mixes its presence with his every plan. So far all is passive. But besides this he plans and contrives for that other's happiness; tries to devise what would give pleasure; examines his own conduct and conversation, to avoid that which can by any possibility give pain. This is meditation.

So, too, is meditation on religious truth carried on. If it first be loved, it will recur spontaneously to the heart. Meditation is done in silence. By it we renounce our narrow individuality, and expatiate into that which is infinite. Only in the sacredness of inward silence does the soul truly meet the secret, hiding God. The strength of resolve, which afterward shapes life and mixes itself with action, is the fruit of those sacred, solitary moments. There is a Divine depth in silence. We meet God alone. Have we never felt how a human presence, if frivolous, in such moments frivolizes the soul, and how impossible it is to come in contact with any thoughts that are sublime, or drink in one inspiration from heaven, without degrading it, even though surrounded by all that would naturally suggest tender and awful feelings, when such are by? It is not the number of books you read; nor the variety of sermons which you hear; nor the amount of religious conversation in which you mix : but it is the frequency and the earnestness with which you meditate on these things, till the truth which may be in them becomes your own, and part of your own being, that ensures your spiritual growth.

> The thought of God, the thought of Thee,
>   Who liest in my heart,
> And yet beyond imagined space
>   Outstretched and present art,—
> The thought of Thee, above, below,
>   Around me and within,
> Is more to me than health and wealth,
>   Or love of kith and kin.

BE favorable to us, O Lord! and increase in our hearts the feelings of piety and devotion with which Thou hast inspired us; and for fear that the inconstancy and cowardice so natural to us may chill our fervor, mercifully grant us the aid we need to conquer all that is in opposition to our love for Thee, and to serve Thee with all the fidelity we owe Thee, never relaxing in our duty to Thee. We beg this through the merits and mediations of Jesus Christ Thy Son our Lord. *Amen.*

Second Tuesday.

Let the wicked forsake his way, and the unrighteous man his thoughts: and let him return unto the Lord, and He will have mercy upon him; and to our God, for He will abundantly pardon.

Except ye repent, ye shall all likewise perish.

VERY seriously, very severely, does our Lord Jesus Christ deal with the sins of His people. He suffers no man to make light of sin. If His Word, if conscience, if the Spirit's striving, suffices not, then a sterner discipline begins to chasten,—pain and loss and shame and punishment; perhaps at last a blighted name, ruined prospects, deposition from service, deprivation of usefulness,—anything rather than that the soul should be lost; anything rather than that the man should sleep the sleep of death. These things are the reproofs of Christ: As many as I love, He says, I rebuke and chasten. Gospel regrets are reparations too.

But language is sometimes used as to the consequences of sin, which seems calculated rather to depress than to stimulate the energies of true repentance. A young man is told, for example, that the consequences of one evil thought are essentially interminable; that each particular word carries an influence with it never to be checked and nowhere to be bounded; that the smallest omission of duty, much more the smallest act of transgression, not only has in it a condemning sentence, but also exercises (whatever he *may* be afterward) an absolutely illimitable and everlasting force. And there is a truth in such representations. The consequences of sin are incalculable. The transgressor himself has no power to say to his own evil: Thus far shalt thou go, and no further. The thing done or the thing left undone—the word spoken or the thought cherished—is out of his hand: he cannot revoke and he cannot regulate it. This is true. But such representations, left alone, can but make man reckless. I have more faith in the opposite truth. The long suffering of Jesus Christ not only reproves but will in part repair also: as *with every temptation God will also make a way to escape*, so (in some sense) beside every sin He sets a repentance and a reparation.

I know not, on this side the grave, the spot from which repentance, nay, from which reparation, is excluded. Repentance is reparation. The man who, far on in life's journey, has sinned and fallen, makes reparation toward man if he repents toward God. The servant of God, who has been ensnared of evil,—who has even brought shame upon his name, and reproach upon his Church,—yet even he, if he returns and repents; even he, if he walks humbly and mournfully for his remaining days before God; even he, if he accepts with unmurmuring submission that sentence of comparative uselessness which is the worst part of sin, and is willing to stoop to humble work, and to be but *a hewer of wood and drawer of water* for that tabernacle in which perhaps once he stood a priest ministering; even he, if he comes back—it is no imaginary picture—just to die amongst his people, making no secret of his grief and of his repentance, and readily offering up the remnant of a shortened life upon the sacrifice and service of a penitent restitution; even that man has upon him the mark of forgiveness, is clad again with the white garments of a second absolution, and when he goes hence, to be no more seen of the sinful, shall enter, washed and justified, within the innermost veil, to be forever a king and a priest in that sanctuary where sin is not. That in me first Jesus Christ might show forth all longsuffering!

> A broken heart, O God, my King,
>   Is all the sacrifice we bring :
> Thou, God of grace, wilt not despise
>   A broken heart in sacrifice.

O GOD of compassion, God of pity, God who, according to the multitude of Thy great mercies, washest away the sins of the penitent, and by the grace of remission doest away the guilt of past offences; look graciously upon Thy servants, and hearken unto them entreating for the forgiveness of all their sins; through our Lord Jesus Christ. *Amen.*

Third Wednesday.

Then saith He unto them, My soul is exceeding sorrowful, even unto death: tarry ye here, and watch with Me. And He went a little farther, and fell on His face, and prayed, saying, O my Father, if it be possible, let this cup pass from Me: nevertheless not as I will, but as Thou wilt. And He went away again the second time, and prayed, saying, O my Father, if this cup may not pass away from Me, except I drink it, Thy will be done. And He left them, and went away again, and prayed the third time, saying the same words.

THERE is very often some one special darling evil thing around which the will is found to wind and fasten itself with passionate clinging. It does not say aloud, but it would if it were frank, "This I cannot give up; this I must have." Of course the object is different with each of us; but the sin is the same. It cannot be safe to live with such a reservation as that. That soul offends in the one point, but breaks the unity of the whole law, and this makes it "guilty of all." It is setting up an idol in our hearts; and then we may be sure God sets Himself, not in any arbitrary way, not in jealousy of our joy, but in the very love wherewith He loves us, and that He may give us all heaven at last, to take the idol out. We yield, unwillingly perhaps, at first, though in that case the pain will only be so much the greater. But by all means, at any rate, by ways that we had not known, by dealings that perplex and confound us, He begins to loosen the fatal fascination and take it away.

> The Infinite, who sees us thus
>   Mould His transcendent form in clay,
> Shatters the idol into dust,
>   And we, alas! must weep and pray.

But first, in His tenderness, He always calls to us by voices of prophets, by mercies, sermons, prophecies, providences,—"Give Me thine heart." It is not to be concealed that, in this final surrender, as in all the others, from the first glowing hour of a new-born affection for the Lord, the heart led the way toward the foot of the Cross. But the will, too, bears a part, consenting and helping, as it were, by solemn purposes and exertions, to bend itself to the will of God, with renunciation and submission. Only, it must be remembered, here comes in that new and really supernatural gift of the Spirit of God, which makes this act of the will different from every other. No man can tell exactly where the line runs that divides man's part from God's in spiritual renewing and growth. But this we know, for God and our hearts both tell it to us, that "God worketh in us both to will and to do," and yet it is not till *we* both "will" and "do," that the blessed work is done. Perhaps the truth is best expressed by saying that we *will* to lean ourselves on God, and be thus upheld. A traveller of no great strength undertakes to climb Mount Washington. He comes presently to the end of his power and his breath, and sinks down exhausted; but he does not despair. A stronger friend comes to his side, but instead of stirring him up and compelling him to a fruitless struggle, or urging him on, offers to let him lean on his arm. Here is a new opportunity for the exercise of the traveller's will. He is not passive; he *wills to lean* and be helped, and at the same time he wills to use all the power he has. And so he comes to the top, with nothing above him but the heavens.

The submission that makes no merit of its cross; that does not venture to choose one lighter than the Lord lays on us; that does not seek the ability to bear it in the delirium of pleasure, or the drugs of the world, or the deadening influence of time and change; that does not compare your cross with those borne by others, or ask an explanation of it till the day break and the shadows flee away, but bears it all with a child's love for His sake who did not impose it till He had borne all the might and sharpness of all the world's crosses together,—this is the victory. The earth has no fatal fear and no insupportable sorrow in it after you have come to this; you are free in a boundless liberty, strong in immortal strength, and at peace in a peace too deep for the understanding to explain, or any sufferings to disturb.

> Full many a throb of grief and pain
>   Thy frail and erring child must know;
> But not one prayer is breathed in vain,
>   Nor does one tear unheeded flow.
>
> Thy various messengers employ;
>   Thy purposes of love fulfil;
> And 'mid the wreck of human joy,
>   Let kneeling faith adore Thy will.

O MOST merciful Lord, who healest the inward man by outward afflictions, and by troubles in this world dost prepare us for eternal joys in the world to come; by that cup of sorrow which Thou drankest for us, and by that weary path which Thou troddest, grant that we may willingly drink of Thy cup, and cheerfully follow Thee along the road where Thou hast gone before; who with the Father and the Holy Ghost reignest one God, world without end. *Amen.*

Third Thursday.

Mary hath chosen that good part, which shall not be taken away from her.

O tarry thou the Lord's leisure; be strong, and He shall comfort thine heart; and put thou thy trust in the Lord.

LET us excite each other to seek that good part which shall not be taken away from us. Let us labor to be really in earnest, and to view things in the way in which God views them. Then it will be but a little thing to give up the world; but an easy thing to reconcile the mind to what at first it shrinks from. Let us turn our mind heavenward; let us set our thoughts on things above, and in His own time God will set our affections there also. All will in time become natural to us, which at present we do but own to be good and true. We shall covet what at present we do but admire. Let the time past suffice us to have followed our own will; let us desire to form part of that glorious company of Apostles and Prophets, of whom we read in Scriptare. Let us cast in our lot with them, and desire to be gathered about their feet. Let us beg of God to employ us; let us try to obtain a spirit of perfect self-surrender to Him, and an indifference to one thing above another in this world, so that we may be ready to follow His call whenever it comes to us. Thus shall we best employ ourselves till His voice is heard, patiently preparing for it by meditation, and by looking for Him to perfect what, we trust, His own grace has begun in us.

There are many persons who proceed a little way in religion, and then stop short. God keep us from choking the good seed, which else would come to perfection! Let us exercise ourselves in those good works which both reverse the evil that is past, and lay up a good foundation for us in the world to come.

> He liveth long who liveth well!
>   All other life is short and vain;
> He liveth longest who can tell
>   Of living most for heavenly gain.
>
> He liveth long who liveth well!
>   All else is being flung away;
> He liveth longest who can tell
>   Of true things truly done each day.

THIRD THURSDAY.

O LORD Jesus Christ, who hast said, My Father worketh hitherto, and I work ; grant us, we beseech Thee, such zeal in Thy service, that we may never be weary in well doing, but may labor steadfastly unto the end through Thy mercy. *Amen.*

Third Friday.

Christ Jesus, whom God hath set forth to be a propitiation through faith in His Blood.

I, even I, am He that blotteth out thy transgressions for Mine own sake, and will not remember thy sins.

God is Love; the assertion, to our exceeding comfort, is twice solemnly made in Holy Scripture. Nothing can exceed the tenderness of the tie which binds Him to every one of His rational creatures, who are His spiritual offspring; no affection or sympathy, of which human life gives us experience, can at all adequately express to us the yearning, self-sacrificing devotion which the Father of spirits entertains toward all the souls He has created, however far they may have wandered from Him into the mazes of sin and error. The Atonement was effected by a Person in the Godhead, and has all the incalculable value which such an agency can give it. He took human nature into conjunction with His divine nature, and thus *atoned* (or reconciled) God and man, as the first step in His gigantic enterprise. In the creature nature which it pleased Him to assume, He offered to the Father a perfectly holy and devoted human life, a life of perfect and intense love and purity, and therefore infinitely acceptable to Him, who is Love and Purity. But in doing so, He entangled Himself in the rancorous hostility and persecution of those He came to save; and thus furnished an evidence, not only of God's willingness to save them, but of their utter alienation from God. And, as He thoroughly identified Himself with our nature, He entangled Himself also in all the distressing consequences of our sin,—hardship, pain, bereavement, death; and—what was to Him more distressing than all—the clouding over of the soul, by the withdrawal from it of that sense of Divine favor which is its sunlight. But the crush and pressure of these awful trials only brought out the perfume of His graces. He was full of love still, even when stretched in agony upon the Cross, of forgiving love, restoring love, sympathizing love, to man; of acquiescing, resigned, confiding love toward God. "Father, forgive them;" "Father, remove this cup from me; nevertheless not as I will, but as Thou wilt;" "Father, into Thy hands I commend my spirit,"—these were the dominant chords of His state of mind, in the course of a trial the severity of which none but Himself and God could appreciate. Now, surely it is not hard to understand that such a life and such a death must have been supremely acceptable to God, and, being rendered by One who took our common nature upon Him, and appeared as our Representative, must have entirely met and discharged what I may call the demands of God's perfect holiness in the acceptance of sinners.

> Though long the weary way we tread,
>   And sorrows crown each lingering year,
> No path we shun, no darkness dread,
>   Our hearts still whispering, Thou art near!
>
> On Thee we fling our burdened woe,
>   O Love Divine! for ever dear;
> Content to suffer while we know,
>   Living and dying, Thou art near!

O GOD, who of Thy great love to this world didst reconcile earth to heaven through Thine only-begotten Son, grant that we who, by the darkness of our sins, are turned aside from brotherly love, may by Thy light shed forth in our souls be filled with Thine own sweetness, and embrace our friends in Thee, and our enemies for Thy sake, in a bond of mutual affection; through Jesus Christ our Saviour. *Amen.*

Third Saturday.

It is a good thing to show forth thy faithfulness every night. Where is God my Maker, who giveth songs in the night?
By His light I walked through darkness.

St. Athanasius observes that, from the creation of the world until Christ, the day preceded the night, as we read in Scripture; but from the coming of Christ, the night precedes the day; and thus we begin to celebrate the day solemnly from the evening of the preceding day. This was typical to show how from light men were to decline to darkness, from God to errors and idolatry; but from the time that the Sun of Justice—Christ—rose upon us, we are brought out of darkness into the light of Divine faith. Anna, the widow, departed not from the temple day and night; the holy shepherds, too, were keeping watch when they beheld the vision of angels in the sky; and the Saviour himself repeatedly reminds us of the need of watching by night, and taught us by His example, and admonished Peter in the time of the Passion: "Couldst thou not watch one hour?" Know, therefore, that vigils are agreeable to God.

Nothing is constant with men. Everything revolves and perishes. Alas! we proposed to perform great things when the sun was mounted to the meridian, and lo! in a short time, it descends to evening. The day is become old, the night is approaching; such is the frailty of this mortal life. How soon the day declines, the heat cools, the light sinks and is buried in the shade of evening; but we must run our course until we shall behold the Lord of lords in Sion.

It is the vesper hour. What a symbol is here! Let us say, therefore, with the disciples, whose hearts burned within them by the way: "Abide with us, for it is toward evening." Now evening, the mother of night, will bring forth darkness; now sadness oppresses us, and despair sinks. The waters have come even unto our soul; the cold of iniquity freezes us, and a wounded conscience dreads the terrible sentence of the Judge. Abide with us, O most clement Lord, since without Thee we can do nothing; we are nothing! Thou art our consolation, Thou art our refuge and strength; Thou art a tower of might against the face of our enemies. The night of wickedness covers all things; the light of truth faileth; depravity abounds; charity grows cold; our eyes are turned to Thee, that we may not perish. Abide with us, that the darkness may not come upon us, and that the shining light which shineth to us in that dark place may not be extinguished in the night. The end of life is near; the evening of our day; deliver us from the power of darkness, and turn not in anger from Thy servants; because if Thou art with us, we shall fear no evil in the midst of the shadow of death, but with the brightness of Thy grace we shall be enlightened in that region of the dead. It is good to be with Thee, O Jesus. Abide with us, and turn not away from us. The darkest night draws on, in which no man can work. Abide with us, and close the door upon us, until the darkness shall pass over, and light again rise to visit us.

> Lead kindly Light, amid the encircling gloom,
> Lead Thou me on;
> The night is dark, and I am far from home,
> Lead Thou me on:
> Keep Thou my feet, I do not ask to see
> The distant scene; one step enough for me.

LIGHTEN our darkness, we beseech Thee O Lord; and by Thy great mercy defend us from all perils and dangers of this night for the love of Thy only Son our Saviour Jesus Christ. *Amen.*

Third Sunday.

Above all things have fervent charity among yourselves.
The love of Christ constraineth us.
Ye yourselves are taught of God to love one another.
This is my commandment, That ye love one another, as I have loved you.

CHRIST does not say that all persons are to be loved by us alike,—with equal degrees of personal interest and attachment; for He never asks what cannot be. But that kind of love which springs from our being all one in Him whose boundless love embraces all for the sake of redeeming them unto eternal blessedness and gladness, unworthy as they are,—this is possible for us toward every child of God; the unsightliest, the most disagreeable, the least lovely, the worst. We cannot reverse the inwrought laws of taste, attraction, preference, common culture and common life, which group and distribute men. But we can merge them all in that one common charity which, in the Redeemer himself, was large enough to reach and gather up the vilest, and which in His true followers can see in every human creature this trace of nobleness and beauty—the capacity of being by repentance and faith raised to heavenly places—of wearing the likeness and the righteousness of the Lord forever and forever. In other words, all can be loved in Him, and will be by those that have their life in Him. And we must not be too fastidious about people forsaking their ugliness and correcting their faults, before our charity goes out to them. Suppose a moment the grace of God had been measured to us by that thrifty rule.

> Look long at Jesus; His sweet blood,
> How was it dealt to thee!

A child asked: "When God blots out the sins on our souls, are the blots left?" So no material image suffices to display the marvellous condescension and grace of God's charity in His Son. But this we know,—He does not look at the blots. The figure is but of robes, and they are washed and made white in the blood of our justification and pardon. How true it is, then, that the grace of charity, like all other graces, has its roots in the one common ground of Christ's own spiritual life; that all the branches through one living trunk unite there.

> I in your care my brethren left,
> Not willing ye should be bereft
>   Of waiting on your Lord.
> The meanest offering ye can make—
> A drop of water—for love's sake,
>   In heaven, be sure, is stored.

O CHRIST Thou living fire, kindle within me the fire of Thy love, which Thou didst shed abroad in the earth; that it may remove all vice from my soul; that it may purify my conscience from remorse; that it may cleanse my body from all sin; and that it may kindle the light of the knowledge of Thee in my heart, for thine own dear sake. *Amen.*

Third Monday.

Not as though I had already attained, either were already perfect.

This one thing I do, forgetting those things which are behind, and reaching forth unto those things which are before, I press toward the mark for the prize of the high calling of God in Christ Jesus.

THERE is an oblivion of the irreparable which is at once true and salutary. The past is. No regrets, no tears, no repentances, can make it undone. Then accept it, recognize it, start from it. Do not expect to be that which your individual history forbids that you should be. God sees you as you are; see yourself so. God knows by what gradual steps of sin you have fallen to this estate; God knows by what gradual steps of repentance you have risen to this. Such as you are, be such,—such when you kneel before your God,—such when you go abroad among men! *Forget the things behind.* That which you cannot be, by reason of your sin, dismiss it. That which you cannot be, by reason of your sin, forget it. If there is something which you cannot be, there is something also which you can be. If you cannot be a saint, you may be a penitent; if you cannot sit on the right hand or sit on the left, at least you may yet be a hired servant; at least you may be yet a doorkeeper in the House of your God. Rest there, and be thankful. Merely to dwell among the thoughts of what might have been is unreal, and therefore unprofitable. Learn, secondly, and on the other hand, the oblivion of the attained. That is it of which St. Paul speaks. He counts not himself to have apprehended; in that sense chiefly he forgets the things behind. The experience of life makes us almost weary of the records of Christian experience as now received. If I had my choice—a man is *tempted* to say—I would dwell rather with the irreligious. There at least I shall find reality; I shall find naturalness; I shall find humility. There we hear nothing about "humble instruments," nor about being privileged to do a work for God. There are no publications of the triumphs of self-sacrifice, nor of the wonderful achievements wrought by the first appearance, in the home of the ungodly, of the saintly man or the gifted woman. Ah! how different was it in the first days! Where in St. Paul's Epistles do we find anything which offends thus the palate of taste, or thus grates upon the ear of modesty? There, on the contrary, we find an utter self-forgetfulness, a remembrance honestly made of sins, and a hearty sense that Christ is all, and that whatever is, is of Him. We have got the *words*, and too much of them; but we have lost the feeling and the thing signified. The minister of Christ must tell his triumphs on the platform; and the woman who may not preach Christ in churches must preach herself through the medium of the narrative, the memoir, or the autobiography.

Forget, St. Paul says, *the things behind*. If God has enabled you to win back your own soul from evil,—or to save a brother's soul from death, —thank Him for it, and then forget it. If you, who were once the slave of sin, have become through Divine grace able to see and to follow the light of life and of immortality, stay not to reflect upon it; press on, linger not, that you may not only enjoy the foretaste, but also win the crown. When St. Paul forgot the things behind, think what there was in it. He had seen Jesus Christ, and received from His own lips the Apostolic mission. He had left all, and followed Him. He had demolished by a stroke the whole fabric of an almost completed self-righteousness, and set out quite afresh in a race of self-denial, self-sacrifice, and self-crucifixion. And yet he forgot all this. What have we to forget? Where, in our case, is the edifice of the natural virtue? Where, in our case, is the achievement of the spiritual grace? If it be there, it is to be forgotten; if it be not there, who shall measure the depth of the just, the Christian self-abasement?

> No longer forward nor behind
> I look in hope and fear;
> But, grateful, take the good I find,
> The best of now and here.
>
> Enough that blessings undeserved
> Have marked my erring track—
> That wheresoe'er my feet have swerved,
> His chastening turned me back.

O GOD, who bestowest this upon us by Thy grace, that we should be made righteous instead of ungodly, blessed instead of miserable; be present to Thine own works, be present to Thine own gifts; that they in whom dwells a justifying faith may not lack a strong perseverance, through Jesus Christ our Lord. *Amen.*

Third Tuesday.

In that He suffered being tempted, He is able to succor them that are tempted.

For we have not an high-priest which cannot be touched with the feeling of our infirmities; but was in all points tempted like as we are, yet without sin. Let us therefore come boldly to the throne of grace, that we may obtain mercy, and find grace to help in time of need.

I suppose no truth can be dearer to a human heart than these two,—the sympathy of the Son of Man in temptation, the victory of humanity in the Son of Man over evil. For we are so tried and tossed, so compassed around with pain, so much apparently the sport of fanciful passion, so curiously framed as it were for temptation, with high aspirations living in us along with base desires; so hovering ever on the verge of good and ill, and so weak to choose the good; so troubled by the necessity of battle when our heart is weary with the passionate longing for rest; so sick of ourselves and of the vile cravings which at times possess us, —that God knows we do want some sympathy higher than any one on earth can give us,—some sympathy which will not weaken but strengthen; some certainty that the Eternal Love and Righteousness can feel with us and assist us. Therefore it is the deepest blessedness to know that One who shared in our nature—the proper Divine Man— was in the days of His flesh a partaker of "our strong crying and tears," and "learned obedience by the things which He suffered," for then we know that He can, in His triumphant nature, be still "touched with the feeling of our infirmities." Brethren, who are struggling with evil within you and without, you have with you the exalting power-bestowing sympathy of the Son of God and Son of Man. Another consoling truth is that humanity has conquered evil. Take that great fact as the foundation of all action. There has been human temptation without human fall. There has been one Man at least who has met sin on its own ground and has baffled the tempter. He is your own Brother and your God. Sin is at His feet, and death and hell. Brethren, if we love Him, they shall be at ours. We look forward, then, not to defeat, but to victory,—to individual victory, to universal victory. The conquest in the wilderness is the earnest of a greater conquest yet to be. Ah! why should we faint and falter and despair, when that is so divinely true? We are fellow-workers with the Almighty Goodness to that majestic end. Therefore, conquer evil in yourselves in the strength of Christ. Personally, that is the only thing worth living for. And once you have begun to conquer evil in your own heart, you will be able to contend to the death against evil without you in the world. Let us pray with added fervor that He who fought and won the battle in the wilderness may give us power to do our duty against all wrong and all sin, with our whole heart and soul and mind and strength.

> Confirm us in each good resolve;
> The tempter's envious rage subdue;
> Turn each misfortune to our good;
> Direct us right in all we do.

O LORD God of infinite mercy, who hast sent Thy Holy Son into the world to redeem us from intolerable misery; let my faith, I beseech Thee, be the parent of a good life, a strong shield to repel the fiery darts of the devil; and grant that I may be supported by its strength in all temptations, and refreshed by its comforts in all my sorrows, till from the imperfections of this life it may arrive at the consummation of an eternal and never-ceasing love; through Jesus Christ. *Amen.*

Fourth Wednesday.

―― By patient continuance in well doing seek for glory and honor and immortality, eternal life.

Rejoicing in hope; patient in tribulation.

They bring forth fruit with patience.

PATIENCE is of two kinds. There is an active and there is a passive endurance. The former is a masculine, the latter for the most part a feminine grace. Female patience is exhibited chiefly in fortitude; in bearing pain and sorrow meekly without complaining. For the type of man's endurance you may look to the early Christians under persecution. This is the patience for us to cultivate,—to bear and to persevere. However dark and profitless, however painful and weary existence may have become; however any man, like Elijah, may be tempted to cast himself beneath the juniper-tree and say: "It is enough: now, O Lord!"—life is not done, and our Christian character is not won, so long as God has anything left for us to suffer, or anything left for us to do.

Patience, however, has another meaning. It is the opposite of that impatience which cannot *wait*. This is one of the difficulties of spiritual life. We are disappointed if the harvest do not come at once. It is the work of a long life to become a Christian. Many, oh! many a time, are we tempted to say: " I make no progress at all. It is only failure after failure. Nothing grows." Now, look at the sea when the flood is coming in. Go and stand by the sea-beach, and you will think that the ceaseless flux and reflux is but retrogression equal to the advance. But look again in an hour's time, and the whole ocean has advanced. Every advance has been beyond the last, and every retrograde movement has been an imperceptible trifle less than the last. This is progress, to be estimated at the end of hours, not minutes. And this is *Christian* progress. Many a fluctuation, many a backward motion, with a rush at times so vehement that all seems lost,—but if the Eternal work be real, every failure has been a real gain, and the next does not carry us so far back as we were before. Every advance is a real gain, and part of it is never lost. Both when we advance and when we fail, we gain. We are nearer to God than we were. The flood of spirit-life has carried us up higher on the everlasting shores, where the waves of life beat no more, and its fluctuations end, and all is safe at last. "This is the faith and patience of the saints."

> Since thy Father's arm sustains thee,
>   Peaceful be ;
> When a chastening hand restrains thee,
>   It is He.
> Know His love in full completeness
> Fills the measure of thy weakness.
> If He wound thy spirit sore,
>   Trust Him more.

O GOD, who by the passion and death of Thine only-begotten Son didst crush the pride of our enemy the devil ; grant to Thy faithful servants, when they are in trouble, to bear in mind His sufferings, and cheerfully to endure all adversities ; through the same Lord Jesus Christ who livest and reignest with the Father and the Holy Ghost one God, world without end. *Amen.*

Fourth Thursday.

We know that all things work together for good to them that love God.

Knowing this, that the trying of your faith worketh patience. But let patience have her perfect work, that ye may be perfect and entire, wanting nothing.

As the Christian advances upon his way, a sweet and solemn sense of the unity of life grows upon his spirit. "We are complete in Him." Much of our life, if viewed in itself only, would appear purposeless and broken, yet Christ has said: "Gather up these fragments that remain, so that nothing be lost." We learn to look at life as a whole thing; not to be discouraged by this or that adverse circumstance, remembering how much there is and will be in that life which is "like frost and snow, *kindly to the root*, though hurtful to the flower;" fatal to the bloom and fragrance, the lovely and enjoyable part of our nature, but friendly to its true, imperishable life. Looking at ourselves, we may see that, under a slight—sometimes a very slight—modification of inward bent, or outward circumstance, we should have been far more happy, more beloved, *apparently* more useful, than now; yet we may also see as plainly, as we confess it humbly, that we have attained, through all these losses, to that to which every gain is an ever present, appreciable loss. Gradually, almost imperceptibly, the believer will find the current of his existence sweeping into a broader channel; will find "doors opening upon him"—doors of happiness, doors of usefulness—which will be to him a Gate of Heaven; "windows opening," letting in the breath of summer upon his soul, filling it with sunshine and sweet air; suddenly, too, in the deep emergencies of life, some new interest, some friend, will appear like the Great Twin Brethren, or Saint of old, in the thick of the battle, vanishing perhaps when the fight is over, yet blessing him even in vanishing from his sight.

Light is good, and it is a pleasant thing to behold the sun. Yet far dearer than outward peace, far sweeter than inward consolation, is that, the ever-during stay, the solace of the Christian's heart, the imperishable Root of which all else that gladdens it is but the bloom and odor; the dry tree that shall flourish when every green tree of delight and of desire fails. It is to the Cross that the heart must turn for that which will reconcile it to all conflicts, all privations; which will even enable it, *foreseeing them,* to exclaim: "Yet more." When Christ is lifted up within the believing soul, nothing is too hard for it to venture upon or endure; it rests upon a power beyond itself, and can bring its whole strength to bear upon generous, exalted enterprise. Show thy servant *thy work,* and his own will be indeed easy! Let this powerful attraction be once felt, the heart's, the world's great and final Overcoming, and all other bonds will weaken, all other spells decay. "*Midnight is past,*" sings the sailor on the Southern ocean,— "*Midnight is past; the Cross begins to bend.*"

> I do not ask my cross to understand,
>   My way to see—
> Better in darkness just to feel Thy hand,
>   And follow Thee.
> Joy is like restless day, but Peace divine
>   Like quiet night;
> Lead me, O Lord, till Perfect Day shall shine
>   Through Peace to Light.

FOURTH THURSDAY.

ALMIGHTY and everlasting God, who healest us by chastening, and preservest us by pardoning, grant unto Thy suppliants, that we may both rejoice in the comfort of the tranquillity which we desired, and also use the gift of Thy peace for the effectual amendment of our lives; through Jesus Christ our Lord. *Amen.*

Fourth Friday.

And one of the malefactors which were hanged railed on Him, saying, If thou be Christ, save thyself and us. But the other answering, rebuked him, saying, Dost not thou fear God, seeing thou art in the same condemnation? And we indeed justly; for we receive the due reward for our deeds: but this Man hath done nothing amiss. And he said unto Jesus, Lord, remember me when Thou comest into Thy kingdom. And Jesus said unto him, Verily I say unto thee, To day shalt thou be with Me in Paradise.

"REPENT and believe!" is the message of God to fallen man. Some mean to believe without repentance; but they will find themselves mistaken. Faith without previous repentance is a dead thought, a mere notion, a doctrine admitted either with or without evidence,—a weak, second-handed conviction. Reasoning, at the best, built it up; reasoning may pluck it down again. It leaves the mind unenlightened, the heart untouched, unpurified, the life unaltered, the soul under condemnation of death. Faith after true repentance is a conviction resting on experience and intuitive evidence; a truth of the first order; it is the substance of things hoped for and the unshaken evidence of things unseen by carnal eyes. It carries reason and logic headlong; it quickens and renews the heart, enlightens the mind, influences the life, overcomes the world, and lays hold on things heavenly and eternal. So was the faith of the penitent sinner: " Lord, remember me when Thou comest into Thy kingdom." How does he come by this faith in circumstances so unspeakably unfavorable, so decidedly opposed to it? The condemned, expiring man, on yonder cross, the Lord of heaven! A stumbling-block of mountain size to the Jews, and the very height of foolishness to the Greeks! His was a giant stretch of faith, I confess. In respect to external support, it outstrips the faith of all the Apostles, the centurion, the distressed fathers and mothers, the blind, the deaf, the lepers, the paralytics; the faith of all martyrs on the stake, in the flames, in persecution, in caves and dens of the earth. It was pure faith, clear and free from every support from without, a work of the Holy Spirit unalloyed by any earthly ingredient. St. Peter walked on the sea,—but he saw Christ pacing with firm steps over the rolling wave. The Apostles remained faithful to their conviction,—but they had witnessed ten thousand exhibitions of Christ's divine power, and had seen Him and conversed with Him for three years. The sick and the distressed came to Him from afar,—but the land was full of His fame. The saints in after times sacrificed their lives for Him,—but they had accumulating proofs of His all-overruling sceptre, daily adding strength (if this be possible) to the testimony of the sacred records. And what is it for us *now* to believe on Him when the cloud of witnesses and the mass of evidence in His favor have already become so boundless that it requires almost a life to pass over and duly estimate the whole of it? It is all comparatively nothing. Our faith is sight; and woe unto that man who can at this present day live and die without being a Christian from his heart! Sodom and Gomorrah, Bethsaida, Chorazin, and Capernaum, the scoffing Jews, the dying impenitent rebel of the text, will condemn him in the judgment day.

Father, perfect my trust!
 Strengthen my feeble faith!
Let me feel as I would when I stand
 On the shores of the River of Death—

Feel as I would were my feet
 Even now slipping over the brink;
For it may be I'm nearer home,
 Nearer now than I think.

O THOU, who showest mercy and pity, grant me that through true faith, through good works, and through the Communion of Thy Holy Body and Blood, I may come to Thee at last; and have mercy on Thy creatures, and on me a great sinner; who reignest with the Father and the Holy Ghost one God world without end. *Amen.*

Fourth Saturday.

Let not your heart be troubled, neither let it be afraid. In every thing by prayer and supplication with thanksgiving let your requests be made known unto God. And the peace of God, which passeth all understanding, shall keep your hearts and minds through Christ Jesus.

The right method of dealing with anxieties, and maintaining peace of heart under them, is clearly and succinctly laid down by St. Paul in this precept. Whatever may be your wishes on the subject which makes you anxious, refer them to God in prayer (using the simplest and most direct language), not asking Him absolutely to bring them about, which might be productive of anything but a happy result, but simply letting him know them, and begging Him to deal in the matter, not according to your short-sighted views, but as seems best to His wisdom and love. If prudence and caution dictate that anything should be done to avert the evil you anticipate, do it, and then think no more of the subject. Thinking of it is utterly fruitless: "Which of you by taking thought can add one cubit unto his stature?" And fruitless thinking is just so much waste of that mental and spiritual energy, every atom of which you need for your spiritual progress. Deal with a fruitless anxiety as you would deal with an impure or a resentful motion of the heart. Shut the door on it at once, and with one or two short ejaculatory prayers, rouse the will and turn the thoughts in a different direction. The holy women on their road to Christ's sepulchre anticipated a difficulty which threatened to baffle entirely their pious design. "Who shall roll us away the stone," they said among themselves, "from the door of the sepulchre?" It turned out that they were troubled about nothing. When they marched up close to it, the difficulty had vanished. "When they looked," says the Evangelist, "they saw that the stone *was* rolled away." Take encouragement from their example. Go forward in your spiritual course with all the energy of your soul. Place the foreseen difficulties in the hand of God, and He shall remove them.

Those who indulge fretful feelings, either of anxiety or irritation, know not what an opening they thereby give to the devil in their hearts. "Fret not thyself," says the Psalmist; "*else shalt thou be moved to do evil.*" And in entire harmony with this warning of the elder Scriptures is the precept of St. Paul against undue indulgence of anger: "Let not the sun go down upon your wrath, *neither give place to the devil.*" Peace is the sentinel of the soul, which keeps the heart and mind of the Christian through Christ Jesus. So long as this sentinel is on guard and doing his duty, the castle of the soul is kept secure. But let the sentinel be removed, and the way is opened immediately for an attack upon the fortress. And our spiritual foes are vigilant, however much we may sleep. They are quick to observe an opportunity, and prompt to avail themselves of it. They rush upon the city at once in the absence of the sentinel, and do great mischief in a short time.

In conclusion, be careful to maintain peace in the heart, if thou wouldst not only resist the devil, but also receive the guidance of God's Spirit. That Spirit cannot make communications to a soul in a turbulent state, stormy with passion, rocked by anxiety, or fevered with indignation. The Lord is neither in the great and strong wind, nor in the earthquake, nor in the fire; and not until these have subsided and passed away, can His still small voice be heard communing with man in the depths of his soul.

<blockquote>
If our love were but more simple
We should take Him at His word;
And our lives would be all sunshine
In the sweetness of our Lord.
</blockquote>

O LORD, we beseech Thee to grant unto Thy people such a measure of Thy heavenly benediction and grace, that by the continuance of Thy clemency they may be delivered in every hour of need from the weakness of the flesh and the malice of the devil; through Jesus Christ our Lord. *Amen.*

Fourth Sunday.

Ho, every one that thirsteth, come ye to the waters, and he that hath no money; come ye, buy, and eat; yea, come, buy wine and milk without money and without price.

Let him that heareth say, Come. And let him that is athirst come. And whosoever will, let him take the water of life freely.

Eat, O friends; drink, yea, drink abundantly, O beloved.

THOU art invited, O my soul, to a royal banquet; put on thy best apparel then, for the King that bids thee will take great notice of thy dress. It is the marriage supper of the great King; let me, then, get on the wedding garment, that I may go out to meet the Bridegroom of my soul. Take care that thou appear like a guest, lest the Lord of the feast should look upon thee as an intruder. But come, all things are ready. Surely thou dost not stand doubtful whether thou shalt go or not, nor make excuses to put it off till another time? Art thou sure if thou hast rejected this solemn invitation, and refused thy company to the great Master of the feast, who does now so passionately desire it,—art thou sure to be accepted another time? May not these delays provoke the slighted King to cry out in His anger that thou which wert in vain bidden, shalt not taste of His supper?

Raise up thy faculties, therefore, O my soul, and consider the many obligations that thou art under of hastening to the banquet of thy Lord. Think but upon the condescension of the Almighty. He stoops to solicit my presence, and even entreats me to be there; shall I, then, insolently reject these submissions of the Deity, and despise the goodness of my Creator? But as the condescensions of thy Saviour, O my soul, in calling thee to the feast, so the benefits of it to thyself do oblige thee to accept this call, and hasten to the entertainment with an excess of joy. Here is that which conveys grace to the soul, and nourishes my faith and all other virtues to that degree as to make me a new creature, and fit me for the real presence of the Lord in His eternal kingdom. Here is that which ratifies the promises of God, applies the merits of my Redeemer's death to my soul, and, in a word, seals the pardon of my sins. Here is that which will make me, in a manner, the receptacle of my God, for He will come unto me, and make His abode with me; so that I shall enjoy Him here below, and in some measure anticipate His glorious presence, which is in heaven the delight of angels.

Reflect again upon the honor, O my soul, that is conferred upon thee. Why this great honor, O my Lord, to me, the most wretched of all that are called to Thy heavenly table? Was it not enough for Thee to come down from Thy glorious seat above, and die upon the Cross for me, but must Thou also provide this heavenly banquet for Thy servant, and oblige him to sit down in Thy presence, and feed upon the bread of life? O my soul, how I am obliged, in gratitude to my Saviour's love upon the cross, to be frequent in the commemoration of it! He there trod the wine-press of the wicked world's misery, and, in the bitter anguish of His departing soul, cried out that God had forsaken Him. The disgrace as well as the torments of His cruel death, together with His willingness to endure all this for my redemption, are such instances of love, even in this invitation, too, as call for the highest expression of gratitude and a thankful acceptance of the proffer.

FOURTH SUNDAY.

Thine was the bitter price,
  Ours is the free gift given;
Thine was the blood of sacrifice,
  Ours is the wine of heaven!

For Thee the burning thirst,
  The shame, the mortal strife,
The broken heart, the side transpierced;
  To us, the Bread of Life!

GRANT me, blessed Lord, not only to receive that Sacrament in the outward elements, but in the virtue and power thereof; not bread and wine alone, but the Body and Blood of my Jesus, to the remission of all my sins and to all the other benefits of His death and passion for me; through the same Jesus Christ our Saviour. *Amen.*

Fourth Monday.

God, who commanded the light to shine out of darkness, hath shined in our hearts, to give the light of the knowledge of the glory of God in the face of Jesus Christ.

We know that, when He shall appear, we shall be like Him; for we shall see Him as He is.

And every man that hath this hope in him purifieth himself, even as He is pure.

"The angels," says one of the Fathers of the Church, "always carry their heaven about with them wheresoever they are sent, because they never depart from God or cease to behold Him, ever dwelling in the bosom of His immensity, living and moving in Him, and exercising their ministry in the sanctuary of His divinity." Christ gave warrant beforehand to this thought of Gregory the Great, when, speaking of little children, He uttered that unexpected and beautiful description of the privileges of their estate, so unlike all our materialistic ways of reckoning advantages, and says that their angels do always "behold the face of His Father in heaven." The preëminent joy of these spirits that are without the stains of conscious sin is their uninterrupted vision of the beauty of the Lord. The qualification for that honor is purity of heart. Light is thrown from this passage on another, not without its difficulties, where the Saviour seems to make infants models for grown people. The disciples were inquiring who should be greatest in the new kingdom. Such a question must be prompted not merely by a vain curiosity, but by an ambitious emulation. To mortify their calculating selfishness, Jesus placed an infant before them and said, "Whosoever shall humble himself as this little child, the same is greatest in the kingdom of heaven." His other teachings forbid us to understand Him as meaning that children bring into life with them no stains of ancestral evil, and no natural proclivities to falsehood and self-indulgence. Nor can He mean that full grown men and women, fighting in the fierce warfare and suffering in the terrible tragedy of a world of experience, with intellect and will and passion developed, can return to the untried and comparatively passive state of an infantile nature. He rather bids us enter into the spiritual elements of the child's soul, and to find there three or four traits which form essential features of any mature character that wears the holy likeness of His own. One is simplicity. It is the opposite of what we see in so many adult persons in modern society,—a kind of inward conspiracy between intense selfishness and an unscrupulous intellect; a strong head combined with a bad heart. This is something that in a child would be pronounced morally monstrous. Another trait is docility,—a readiness to receive wisdom, whether taught by authority or shining by its own light. This is the quality that gives its signification to the word disciple,—the chosen name of the learners in Christ's school. Another trait is trustfulness. This is the willingness to be led on and held up by a stronger hand. It is the childish germ of that great power in the Christian which afterward, under the nurture of the Gospel at the foot of the Cross, accepts the Divine mysteries, believes what passes the understanding, renounces self-sufficiency, and inherits the victories that are promised to faith. Another yet is purity. This is a cleanness from those actual defilements that come by the personal indulgence of the lusts of the flesh. It belongs to hearts that are either unpolluted by the touch of external corruption, or else, by the purifying power of the Holy Spirit, after having been once disordered through the inordinate activity of the senses, are restored to chastity. These, then, are the spiritual graces that we are to cultivate, or to restore in our souls if we would share in the benediction pronounced by the Saviour on a child-like character. If we inquire which is chief among them, some light is thrown on that question when we turn to the Beatitudes. What is the grace that is there specially singled out as the qualification for the Beatific Vision? "Blessed are the pure in heart, for they shall see God." The meek shall inherit the earth. Hunger and thirst after righteousness shall have their longing filled. The merciful shall obtain more mercy than they bestow. The peace-makers shall be called God's children. But there is one measure of the fulness of joy higher and richer than any other. It is not only to be rewarded and comforted by being in heaven, but it is, with the angels that watch over little children, to SEE Him whose presence makes it heaven. Among all the raptures of beatitude the Beatific Vision is supreme; and that, so far as Revelation has lifted the veil, is only for the pure in heart.

Since to Thy little ones is given such grace,
  That they who nearest stand
Alway to God, in heaven, and see His face,
  Go forth at His command,
Grant, Lord, that when around the expiring world
  Our seraph guardians wait,
While on her death-bed, e'en to ruin hurled,
  She owns Thee all too late;
They to their charge may turn and thankful see
  Thy mark upon us still;
Then all together rise and reign with Thee
  And all their holy joy o'er contrite hearts fulfil!

GIVE me, O Lord, purity of lips, a clean and innocent heart, and rectitude of action. Make me ever to seek Thy face with all my heart, all my soul, all my mind; grant me to have a contrite and humbled heart in Thy presence,—to prefer nothing to Thy love. Most high, eternal, and ineffable Wisdom, drive away from me the darkness of blindness and ignorance; most high and eternal Strength, deliver me; most high and eternal Fortitude, assist me; most high and infinite Mercy, have mercy on me; through Jesus Christ our Lord. *Amen.*

Fourth Tuesday.

Christ reconciling the world unto Himself.

Jesus Christ the righteous: the propitiation for our sins.

God so loved the world, that He gave His only begotten Son, that whosoever believeth in Him should not perish, but have everlasting life.

It is the business of each one of us to apprehend the Gospel of a free, of a personal absolution. "If Jesus Christ took upon Himself the sins of all men, then He took upon Himself my sins—even mine" is an argument not more logically true than individually binding. There must be a personal transaction between God and the soul on this basis. There must be a solemn giving of the individual soul—exactly as it is seen to be and felt to be in history and in circumstance—into the hands of God himself, on the ground of a revelation made by Him in the Gospel as to a free and total forgiveness of all sin through the alone merits of our Lord

Jesus Christ. For lack of this, many men are *all their lifetime subject* still to *bondage*, even though they say with their lips, and hold tenaciously as a doctrine, "I believe in the forgiveness of sins." Yes, but of *whose* sins,—the sins of others, or your own?

Again, it is the business of each one of us to apprehend for himself the Gospel promise of a Holy and Divine Spirit to dwell personally in him as the life of his life and the soul of his soul. *God will give the Holy Spirit to them that ask Him;* then if that be true—if that be true—I have only to ask and I shall receive. This, too, is a transaction between God and the man, which must by its very nature be individual and even secret. God is a lover of acts; and there are acts of the soul as well as acts of the life. It is the business of each one of us, having thus stamped upon himself, by an individual act, the seal of his consecration—the double seal of a Divine absolution and a Divine indwelling—then to go forth as a forgiven man, and as a spiritual man, not indeed to presume upon what he has done,—not indeed to contradict by daily inconsistency, or to sin away by daily trifling, the relation toward God into which he has thus solemnly entered,—but still, I will say it without fear of misconstruction, as much as possible to forget himself; to forget himself in his Saviour's service, and to forget himself in giving his very life for his brethren. Let the individual life, thus far, and in this holy sense, be merged and lost in the relative. Let no cowardly misgiving haunt him, lest perhaps he be going amongst those who share not to the full—or perhaps share not at all—his convictions and his aspirations. Let him go, not asking where he is safest, but who most want him. Let him go, calling in beforehand, and calling in throughout, the forgiving grace and the inhabiting Spirit. Let him go, not to display himself, but to glorify God; leading others, who mark his kind words, his wise counsels, his gracious spirit, his peaceful countenance, to think of his God with more reverence, and of his Saviour with more love. And God *will keep the feet of His saints;* He will not suffer one who thus mixes amongst men to be suddenly surprised or *greatly moved.* Thus, through him not least, shall the Almighty Lord make good His divine saying: *I, lifted up from the earth, will draw all men unto Me.*

For lo! in hidden deep accord,
The servant may be like his Lord.
And Thy love our love shining through
May tell the world that Thou art true,
Till those who see us, see Thee too.

GRANT us, O Lord, not to mind earthly things, but to love things heavenly; and even now, while we are placed among things that are passing away, to cleave to those that shall abide; through Jesus Christ our Lord. *Amen.*

Fifth Wednesday.

If ye will not drive out the inhabitants of the land from before you; those which ye let remain of them shall be pricks in your eyes, and thorns in your sides, and shall vex you in the land wherein ye dwell.

Fight the good fight of faith.

I see another law in my members, warring against the law of my mind, and bringing me into captivity to the law of sin which is in my members.

We are more than conquerors through Him that loved us.

NEVER can it be well with us till we are heartily and boldly at work warring against all the enemies of the King. It may be that one requires our first collected strength and almost undivided attention, but the others must not therefore have peace. We may leave them till they attack us, while we go forward to storm the fenced city of another, but we must make no friendship with them, nor even let them come peaceably to us. They are against our God, and we must be against them, or we cannot be wholly for Him.

We Christians are His soldiers, and must not shrink from carrying out His orders. If we make terms with sin, we are traitors to Him who requires that we should be ready even to resist unto blood, and proclaims, "He that findeth his life shall lose it; but he that loseth his life for My sake shall find it." We cannot be as those who have not known Him and His will, nor even as those who rejected Him when they had only seen Him outwardly as the Son of Man, though of them He says that they hated the light, and came not to the light, lest their deeds should be reproved. If we hold off from opening ourselves to His searching, we are like them in not coming to the light; but we are worse, because we say we see, even in a sense in which they did not. They said, "We see," thinking the light of the Law enough. We say we see the light of the Gospel. Worse, then, will it be with us than with them, if we will not come to that light; for any affection we have toward the things it will reprove. Oh, let it shine full upon all your ways! Hold back nothing! Bring every thought, word, look, motion, under its pure and searching light; and wink not when your most favorite fancies and pursuits are before it. Look them through and through, if by any means you may detect in them the least spot of the canker of sin, and when you have found it, magnify it in your own eyes by a concentrated attention as though with a microscope, till you can see its horrid and monstrous shape, and its incalculable growths and multiplications, and till you are not only emboldened to cast it from you, but loathe it, and loathe your very self for having borne it about you.

All that you can see is but a faint image of the malignity that inspires sin, of the spiritual wickedness against which you have to wrestle, and which sets itself utterly and wholly against God, and against all that is good and holy, and would turn the whole creation into loathsomeness and corruption. With this you take part, so far as you allow sin. For your soul's sake, and for the love of your Creator, your Redeemer, your Sanctifier, beware of such fellowship!

> Thou treadst upon enchanted ground;
> Perils and snares beset thee round;
> Beware of all; guard every part,
> But most, the traitor in thy heart.

Come, then, my soul! now learn to wield
The weight of thine immortal shield;
Put on the armor from above
Of heavenly truth and heavenly love.

O LORD, the great Physician of our mortal hurts and wounds, send, we beseech Thee, Thy salvation upon our weakness, that with Thee on our side and fighting for us we may overcome the assaults of the enemy, and, pouring forth all our tears and sorrows before Thee, may prevail against the motions of our sins; through Thy mercy who livest and reignest with the Father and the Holy Ghost one God, world without end. *Amen.*

Fifth Thursday.

It is enough for the disciple that he be as his master, and the servant as his lord.

Even as the Son of man came not to be ministered unto, but to minister, and to give His life a ransom for many.

He died for all, that they which live should not henceforth live unto themselves, but unto Him which died for them and rose again.

Bear ye one another's burdens, and so fulfil the law of Christ.

"Neither the saints here know their own goodness, nor the rejected their own crimes." When Christ the Judge tells them, "Ye treated me so and so," it seems strange to them, and they both answer, "Lord, when saw we Thee, to be kind or unkind to Thee?" And He will tell them, "Inasmuch as ye did it, or did it not, to one of the least of these My brethren, ye did it, or did it not, to Me." Consider well, Christian friend, what our Lord here teaches us all. He teaches us that He is Himself present with us, in the persons of our brethren, to be well or ill treated. You are out on the road, perhaps, or you are sitting quietly at home, and you meet with some one, or some one comes to you, who needs your help, and you have the power to help him. You refuse, perhaps, to help him, for some selfish reason; perhaps you treat him with rudeness and scorn. He goes away, and you think no more of it. But see what our Lord here teaches concerning you and that person. Your meeting with him will be remembered at the last day, and you will find then, what you little thought of at the time, that it was Christ himself whom you were scorning and rejecting; Christ who laid down His life for you, and who at that and every other moment was giving you all that you had. He asked you for a very little out of His gifts back again: a little money or time or trouble, or may be only a kind word or look, and you refused it.

On the other hand, if you from a sense of duty put yourself out of the way to do another person good in body or soul, though you might not distinctly consider it at the time, you will find at the last that Christ was really there, that He reckons it as if you were doing good to Him: it is written in

His book, and will in nowise lose its reward. Our Lord spake it about bodily charity only; but it holds true also with regard to works of purity, and of that charity which regards people's souls; it seems a trifle, to all but earnest believers, to give way to bad thoughts, to take sinful liberties with the eye or hand; but what says the Scripture? Your eyes and your hands are members of Christ; shall I then take Christ's Eye and Hand, and make an unclean use of them? Indeed, we shall never understand how grievous are our sins against purity, until we have learned to believe indeed that we are members of Christ ourselves; nor against charity, until we believe that our brethren are so. The last day will show us what a depth of good or evil lay in all that we did willingly. It will show us that nothing could be a trifle to us, where there was a right and a wrong.

> If I have turned away,
> From grief or suffering which I might relieve,
> Careless the cup of water e'en to give,
> Forgive me, Lord, I pray,
>
> And teach me how to feel
> My sinful wanderings with a deeper smart;
> And more of mercy and of grace impart,
> My sinfulness to heal.

O GOD, who art Love, grant to Thy children who eat of Thy bread, to bear one another's burdens in perfect good-will; may they with one mind provoke one another to love and to good works, that by their holy conversation the sweet labor of Christ may be shed abroad; through the same Jesus Christ our Lord who reigneth with Thee and the Holy Ghost one God, world without end. *Amen.*

Fifth Friday.

But God forbid that I should glory, save in the Cross of our Lord Jesus Christ, by whom the world is crucified unto me, and I unto the world.

And whosoever doth not bear his cross and come after Me, cannot be My disciple.

Looking unto Jesus, the author and finisher of our faith; who for the joy that was set before Him endured the cross, despising the shame, and is set down at the right hand of the Throne of God.

On whomsoever and howsoever the Cross has come, be it as the evident chastisement of sins, the very consequence of them, or signal punishment for them; yet, if it be borne meekly by virtue of the saving Cross, such—though the poorest or most ignorant, with no other gifts of nature, no speech nor utterance beyond the simple confession of Christ's mercies through the Cross—becomes, by his very being, a preacher of Christ crucified.

Such is the wonderful and mysterious efficacy of the Cross. It has a power and virtue, wherever it descends, infused by Him who said: "When I am lifted up from the earth, I shall draw all men unto Me." Words of comfort have other power, they speak another language, they speak to the heart, when uttered by one who has felt the blessed penetrating, because piercing, touch of the Cross. Words have a power not their own, when given through the inward knowledge of the Cross. They who utter them have a mysterious being and privilege they know not of; of themselves they know this only, that Christ has, as they deeply feel, for their sins, given them His cup to drink. But He who regards not their unworthiness, but has vouchsafed to them His Cross to heal them, giveth to it, in them, its own efficacy. As they on whom His gifts of healing were shown—the lame, or paralytic, or blind, or leprous—became, by their very being, living witnesses of his mighty love, so now, whosoever, having been once blind to himself, to the nature of sin, or the holiness of God, now, through the touch of the Cross, sees; whosoever, once bowed down by a spirit of infirmity to earthly things, has now been lifted up to the Cross, and from it beholds his Lord, is, by that very change, a witness that unto Christ crucified and risen and ascended, " all power is given in heaven and in earth." It needs not words. The lowlier, the more real and powerful his witness; for lowliness is the depth of the grace of Christ. As, before, through sin, there hung around him a nameless something, bearing a token of inward decay, so, when turned to God through the Cross, there is a hidden power within him, giving force to words, looks, acts, his very self-abasement and deep sense of unworthiness, not his own nor known to him, but the presence of the Holy Comforter, who ever rests upon the Cross and hallows it.

Blessed, then, thrice blessed, are ye to whom your Lord has fitted your cross, as He, in His righteous but tender love saw best for you. Blessed are ye, if ye but learn your blessedness, whatever cross, by nature or by the order of His government, He has placed upon you. Ye will not seek high things on whom the lowly Cross has been bestowed. But treasure it up for yourselves in your secret hearts; there is no form of it which is not healing; bury it deep there: it will heal you first, through His gracious Spirit, and when it has healed you, will, through you, heal others. Only yield yourselves to His fatherly hand who gave it you, to do to you, in you, through you, His loving and gracious will. So may the very punishment of sin raise you to the very life of the blessed; the chastisement of self will conform you, by His grace, to His ever-blessed will, which is the joy of angels, the perfection of saints, the bond of all things, the end of the human life.

> Every bird that upward springs
> Bears the Cross upon his wings;
> We without it cannot rise
> Upward to our native skies.
>
> Every ship that meets the waves
> By the Cross their fury braves;
> We, on life's wide ocean tost,
> If we have it not are lost.
>
> Hope it gives us when distressed,
> When we faint it gives us rest;
> Satan's craft and Satan's might
> By the Cross are put to flight.

O ADORABLE Jesus, of humility and compassion that passeth knowledge, who didst carry Thine own cross to Mount Calvary, and didst bid the mourners who followed Thee not to weep for Thee, but for themselves! grant me to be a partaker of Thy spirit, that I may bear with a patient mind whatever cross Thou shalt lay upon me, and bewail with true repentance my transgressions, so that, crucified to the world, I may be quickened by Thy cross to life everlasting. Grant this, Lord Jesus, for Thine own mercy's sake. *Amen.*

Fifth Saturday.

The kingdom of God cometh not with observation.

Ye therefore, beloved grow in grace, and in the knowledge of our Lord and Saviour Jesus Christ.

In whom all the building fitly framed together groweth unto an holy temple in the Lord.

As new-born babes, desire the sincere milk of the word, that ye may grow thereby.

MEN grow in stature, they know not how; they eat, they drink, they sleep, are nourished, they know not how; and so, day by day, and year by year, pass through the stages of life, through childhood, youth, to manhood and mature years. So should it be in our recreation. In Holy Baptism, He recreates us in His own image; passes His hand upon us, puts the first germ of spiritual life within us, to grow, be nourished, expand, flower, bear fruit, until it take into itself all our old nature, and we become wholly new. It is a spark from heaven, which should be fanned into a flame by the breath of charity, and burn within us, until it has consumed all low desires, all selfish thoughts, everything which offendeth, and yield us pure, a holy acceptable sacrifice unto God. Such should our Christian course be; such is the blessed course; a gradual daily growth, from the first hour when we awake to the thought of God and of our own deathless being, to our final passage through death to endless life.

By the grace of God alone can we grow; and that flows into us more largely or more scantily according to what we have ourselves become. If we have allowed our hearts to grow cold or worldly, much more if defiled, we cannot at once love or serve God, or repent, or have that alacrity and energy of faith which is the blessing of His more faithful servants. We are not masters of our own faith or love. We cannot expand ourselves to receive God. One step only is in our power,—the next. We cannot at once have great love, or deep humility, or intense penitence, or an active soul, or a reverent spirit, or a devout mind. We can neither at once unlearn evil habits wholly, nor learn great virtues. We can rarely bound in our

Christian course. Step by step is the toilsome ascent to be won. Single acts of virtue, wrought by the grace of God, are the steps to heaven. If in these we correspond to the grace of God, He will give larger increase. It may be He will bring us into some new trial, in which, if by His grace we conquer, He will make us other men. One decisive deed well done, solely for His glory and His love; one trial well surmounted by His grace, will often, through His mercy, lift men up at once far beyond their measure. On one heroic act He has wrought the whole living habit into the soul. A whole life may lie wrapped up in one single deed, which He hath given and crowneth. One fervent act of self-devotion to our Lord, giving ourselves for life or death, weal or woe, to His blessed and almighty will, surrendering ourselves and all which is ours wholly as He wills, and it may be we shall find His gracious hand on ours, leading us to follow His steps, although it be to Calvary. But as this deed or purpose of itself, so all is of grace. The morrow of grace is no more in our power than of time. The first act for which He gives us grace is ours; all beyond is God's. But as we use the present, He will give the future.

Despair we not, then, when we see any grace of reverence or deep love or lowly humility or instant, fervent thankfulness, which we have not; nor yet must we attempt to transplant it at once, full-grown, into ourselves. Pray we for the grace of God to do each single act, as He shall will, to His glory; and He will lead us whither as yet we know not.

> All unseen the Master walketh
>   By the toiling servant's side;
> Comfortable words He speaketh,
>   While His hands uphold and guide.
>
> Holy strivings nerve and strengthen,
>   Long endurance wins the crown;
> When the evening shadows lengthen,
>   Thou shalt lay thy burden down.

O ETERNAL God who seest my weakness and knowest the number and strength of the temptations against which I have to struggle, leave me not to myself, but cover Thou my head in the day of battle, and in all spiritual combats make me more than conqueror through Him that loved me. Grant that I may continue steadfast, immovable, always abounding in the work of the Lord, and, by patient continuance in well-doing, seek, and at last obtain, glory and honor and immortality and eternal life; through Jesus Christ our Lord. *Amen.*

Fifth Sunday.

While we were yet sinners, Christ died for the ungodly, The blood of Jesus Christ cleanseth us from all sin.

Having therefore, brethren, boldness to enter into the holiest by the blood of Jesus, by a new and living way, which He hath consecrated for us, and having an High Priest over the House of God ; let us draw near with a true heart in full assurance of faith.

FEW disciples have ever been brought either to understand the Atonement as a doctrine for the mind, or to feel it as a power in the heart, by any argument. It is not reasoning that brings men to the foot of the Cross. When I know, in my weak will and stricken conscience, that I am worthless, and with no strength in me to make myself rich toward God, I shall want an atonement. When the dreary conviction takes possession of me that I have lost my hold on the mercy-seat in heaven by the thorough selfishness of my life, I shall betake myself to that Mediator who places one of His mighty and merciful hands there, and the other in my own. When I see that, through these wayward or headstrong years, I have so sinned that there is no true life in me, and yet that these years are hurrying away, and that the end is not very far off, I shall be ready to believe in that Sacrifice which takes all sin away,—in that Death which to every believer is endless Life. Then I must say in my closet—and if there, why not openly before the world?—"I am lost if I am left alone. Justify me, O Saviour, through Thy redemption; lay Thy Cross where Thou wilt on this my selfish and sinning nature. Touch me with Thy cleansing blood. Be thou my righteousness, and let me hide myself in Thee."

You believe in God. You know that He is absolutely holy. Before that holiness you know that even angels that are without sin veil their faces. From a contemplation of that splendor of spiritual purity you turn and look upon yourself. Your whole character seems simply one dark spot against the brightness. Reckon it as you will. Look at things done that ought not to have been; look at things left undone that ought to have been done; examine motives and the mixtures of motives; see how much self has had to do with the best things in you; confess that pride and passion have not let you alone, even when you were at your prayers; think of the disguises that your sin has put on, aggravating every other iniquity with that of insincerity; consider what envy and vanity and ambition and lust and anger are, not only in their uncovered deformity, but in the hidden roots of their crafty and unclean life; then reflect what a life *would be* that should render unto God, in blameless obedience and in the unblemished beauty of a holy love, all that is God's, and compare that life with your own. Is not something wanting to bring that soul of yours and God together? Do you not desire a "daysman that can lay his hand upon both?" Is there not needed an atonement? Suppose it is suggested, then, that perhaps, although you are at present so far estranged, you can gradually work your way back and stand by your own endeavor, unatoned or unreconciled, in harmony with your God. Do you believe that? Does your course hitherto, from year to year, look like reaching that consummation? If it did, what security have you of a year or a day to accomplish that great restoration? Besides, what you want is not peace by and by, in an indefinite future; you want it now, if you want it ever. Oh, if every soul that lives forever lives through the Redeemer's dying, then surely this sacrificial redemption is not some abstruse or speculative dogma that we should dispute about it; it is a Divinely human fact, and we are to give thanks for it and glory in it. It is no dream of a troubled sleep, no device of theological ingenuity,—it is the one first and most vital of all living realities to men. It is to be preached as men carry the news of life to their brothers that have been left to die. It is to be believed, without a doubt, by men who, without it, would find life itself darker and drearier than death.

Holy, blessed lives are the fruit of that atonement. So that on this Passion Sunday we can well take up the hymn of the saintly singer of more than two hundred years ago:

> Thou who didst suffer for my good,
>   And die my guilty debts to pay;
> Thou Lamb of God, whose precious blood
>   Can take a world's misdeeds away,—
>
> O let this weary pain, the smart
>   Of life's long tale of grief and loss,
> Be gently stirred within my heart
>   At thought of Thee and of Thy Cross!

I give Thee thanks that Thou didst die,
To win eternal life for me,
To bring salvation from on high :
Oh, draw me up, through love, to Thee!

O BLESSED and adorable Saviour, who didst complete the work of our redemption with many sufferings and woes unutterable! give me grace, I beseech Thee, to follow Thee in the course of Thy bitter passion, that I may consider what Thou didst endure for us sinners ; and be constrained to live henceforth not unto myself, but unto Thee, who didst give Thyself for me, and die, the just for the unjust, to bring me unto God. Grant this for Thy mercy's sake. *Amen.*

Fifth Monday.

If I had not come and spoken unto them, they had not had sin: but now they have no cloke for their sin.

For this cause came I into the world, that I should bear witness unto the truth.

THE words of our Lord Jesus Christ contain many things; but they contain not one compliment; not one word spoken in mere complaisance, in unmeaning acquiescence, in worldly flattery. Whosoever came to Him, friend or foe; whoever invited Him to his house; whoever appealed to Him for His counsel, must make up his mind to being dealt with according to truth. A sinner is a sinner, a hypocrite is a hypocrite, a traitor is a traitor, and as such he is accosted. We scarcely feel, as we read with eighteen centuries between, what a phenomenon this must have been in a world just as flattering then and just as false as now. There was one Person moving upon the earth who evidently took the measure of every life and sounded the depth of every heart; One who could characterize, and made it His business to characterize, each human being who came to Him, exactly as he was, —moral or immoral, sincere or insincere, earnest or indifferent, false or true. No one else could do this justly; no one else could do this with propriety; but there was that in Christ which made men endure it from Him, and though the words might rankle, they must be borne. And the words are there still. The imperishable Book records them. They are written for our admonition. Jesus Christ sees us as we are, and He can only deal with us on a footing of reality.

Some of us have felt the blessing of this. In moments of deep self-conviction, we have found the unspeakable comfort of entering just one only presence in which we are known precisely as we are, and yet are borne with. There is peace, if there be pain also, in the consciousness of that intuition. We have nothing to explain to Jesus Christ. Lie there at His footstool: He knows you through and through, and yet He listens! There is ever peace in truth. If we seek not rest in confession to man, it is partly because it is impossible,

—we cannot, if we would, show ourselves as we are; and partly because we cannot trust man,—could he but see us as we are, he would spurn, he would abhor. But Christ can see,—and yet He loves too.

And the soul feels this. In hours of mirth and gladness, in days of pride and self-ignorance, we may not value Christ either for His truth or for His tenderness. But let the evil day come—it may be of disappointed ambition, it may be of sharp bereavement, it may be (worse yet to bear) of remorse and shame and tarnished honor—then there is something, account for it as we may, which makes the soul trust and turn to the truthful and compassionate Lord; knowing before He speaks that He knows all; knowing before He speaks that He can yet abundantly pardon.

> He is alone my help and hope,
>   That I shall not be moved;
> His watchful eye is ever ope,
>   And guardeth His beloved.
>
> Whether abroad amidst the crowd,
>   Or else within my door,
> He is my pillar and my cloud,
>   Now and for evermore.

BE Thou, O Lord, our protection, who art our redemption; direct our minds by Thy gracious presence, and watch over our path with guiding love; that among the snares which lie hidden in this path wherein we walk, we may so pass onward with hearts fixed on Thee, that by the track of faith we may come to be where Thou wouldest have us; through our Lord Jesus Christ. *Amen.*

Fifth Tuesday.

Let us draw near with a true heart in full assurance of faith, having our hearts sprinkled from an evil conscience.

Though our outward man perish, yet the inward man is renewed day by day.

All the paths of the Lord are mercy and truth unto such as keep His covenant and His testimonies.

They took knowledge of them that they had been with Jesus.

THE work of our sanctification consists simply in receiving, from one moment to another, all the troubles and duties of our state in life as veils under which God hides Himself and gives Himself to us. Every moment brings some duty to be faithfully performed, and this is enough for our perfection. The moment which brings a duty to be performed, or a trouble to be borne, brings also a message declaring to us the will of God. The soul has only to follow Jesus, the Divine Model, by the way of those crosses and sacrifices which every day brings. Are you longing to find out the secret of belonging wholly to God? It is simply this,—to serve Him in all that comes to you; in all that you have to do. All leads to this union; all tends to perfect it, excepting sin, and that which is not our duty. Let us carefully keep hold of the thread of the Divine will; it will guide us through the labyrinth of this life, and bring us safely to the centre, which is God himself.

In the life of faith the soul continually pursues God through all that hides Him, and, if faithful, never stops in this pursuit. All roads bring it nearer to God; all things are means of leading it to Him. Whether God afflicts or comforts the soul, it will equally adore Him to be indeed its Lord and its God. If we had faith, we should be at peace with all creatures, thanking them in our heart for all the sufferings they cause us, because they greatly help to perfect us. The more nature rebels, the more firmly will faith say: "All comes from God, or is allowed by Him, and therefore all is good." There is nothing which faith does not overcome; nothing which it will not accept. Faith passes beyond all earthly things, pierces all shadows, to attain the truth; keeps it ever in a firm embrace, and will never let herself be separated from it. The simplicity and elevation which faith gives to the soul make it satisfied with everything. Nothing is wanting to it; nothing is too much for it; and at all times it blesses the Divine hand which causes the waters of grace to flow so gently upon it. It has the same tenderness for friends and enemies, being taught by Jesus Christ to regard all men as God's instruments. Live as one who is going from the figure to the truth,—from death to immortality, —from time to eternity.

> That love is purest and most true
> Which leans upon its Saviour's breast,
> And thinks with pleasure ever new
> How in all things to please Him best;
>
> Which in all things, not great alone,
> On serving Him is fully bent,
> And knowingly will not to one,
> No! not the smallest sin consent.

O BLESSED Lord, whom without faith it is impossible to please, let Thy spirit, I beseech Thee, work in me such a faith as may be acceptable in Thy sight, even such as may show itself by my works, that it may enable me to overcome the world, and conform me to the image of that Christ on whom I believe; that so at the last I may receive the end of my faith, even the salvation of my soul, by the same Jesus Christ our Lord. *Amen.*

Sixth Wednesday.

Who shall ascend into the hill of the Lord? and who shall rise up in His holy place? He that hath clean hands, and a pure heart.

Follow peace with all men, and *holiness*, without which no man shall see the Lord.

St. Chrysostom, St. Augustine, Bengel, and Tholuck—men that have gone deep down into the sacred significance of the Scriptures—have supposed that by the original word used for *holiness* is meant that special form of holiness or sanctification which consists in the purging away of unchastity. At the root of all the various uses of the term *purity* in the Bible, there lies the idea of a spiritual love unmixed with any baser element. What deranges and poisons the pure relations of human society is an adulterated heart,—the intermixture of sensual with spiritual and orderly affections. When St. Paul exhibits the union of the Church with Christ under the image of the Bride and the Bridegroom, declaring it to be the Divine purpose to present the Bride to her Lord "holy and without blemish," he really offers the strongest conceivable appeal to the Christian disciple for an unspotted life. The holiness to which we are called is not mere moral correctness, such as may result from a cool temperament, or a self-controlling prudence, or a fear of social disgrace, or even a scrupulous conscience. That searching Physician of the heart, who knows all that is in man, aims rather at the inner cleanliness, which is a far more comprehensive and more profound grace, and is obtained only by the creation of his own image in the soul, or rather by a secret union with himself. So St. John, whose own love for his Master was like the colorless light, tells us that the real Christian purity has both its motive and its perfection through an inward reception of Christ by faith and the hope of hereafter being drawn even into a closer communion with Him and likeness to Him. "He that hath this hope in him purifieth himself, even as he is pure." To whatever degree the presence of that immaculate purity is realized, defiled imaginations, thoughts, and actions, become intolerable, and the voluntary indulgence of them becomes impossible. As this refining process goes on—the soul being gradually more and more "changed into the same image, from glory to glory as by the Spirit of the Lord"—it is even conceivable that the whole scene of life where we dwell, with all its moral relationships, should come to be regarded as a kind of sanctuary, and that we should shrink from the pollution of it at any point as instinctively and reverentially as we should from the profanation of a sacrament. This is holiness. At first, and possibly for a long time, it will need incessant vigil and solemn conflict. The forbidden curiosity of the first sinners in Eden tempts us, before we are aware, along the line of their degradation and shame. But, as sure as we are faithful, the struggle will become less sharp. Virtue will find help in the wholesome occupations of a Christian life. The truth will open itself, that a pure religion before God is the busy and charitable religion that visits the fatherless and widow, leaving no time for corrupting trains of thought, reading, or conversation. A spirit so guarded keeps itself unspotted from the world by keeping out of the way of the world's ambiguous allurements. For most of us it is a necessary discipline and a long battle. But even if the faithful soldier and servant should find it a fight unto the life's end, he is not to lose sight of the promised liberty and victory. Advancing well up the hill, he will find that unto the pure all things are pure. Natural objects will be divested of their sensual associations. The entire life will be as unperturbed by passion as the heart is swift in answering to the attractions of Christ's holy will, and perfect in His joy.

> Think that He thy ways beholdeth;
> He unfoldeth
> Every fault that lurks within;
> Every stain of shame glossed over
> Can discover,
> And discern each deed of sin.

O HOLY and immaculate Jesus, who wast conceived in a virgin's womb, and who dost still love to dwell in pure and virgin hearts, give me, I beseech Thee, the grace to keep my heart with all diligence, and to withstand all temptations of the flesh, and with pure and clean heart, to follow Thee the only God, even for Thine own merits and mercy's sake. *Amen.*

Sixth Thursday.

He went out and found others standing idle, and saith unto them, Why stand ye here all the day idle? They say unto Him, Because no man hath hired us.

Then said they unto Him, What shall we do, that we might work the works of God? Jesus answered and said unto them, This is the work of God, that ye believe on him whom He hath sent.

WE complain of the slow, dull life we are forced to lead, of our humble sphere of action, of our low position in the scale of society, of our having no room to make ourselves known, of our wasted energies, of our years of patience. So do we say that we have no Father who is directing our life, so do we say that God has forgotten us, so do we boldly judge what life is best for us, and so by our complaining do we lose the use and profit of the quiet years. We cannot be still, cannot be at rest. It is the most natural and yet the most ruinous fault which belongs to men in an age which lives too fast and has almost a morbid passion for incessant labor. Oh, men of little faith! because you are not sent out yet into your labor, do you think God has ceased to remember you? because you are forced to be outwardly inactive, do you think you also may not be, in your years of quiet, "about your Father's business?" Receive the lesson of Christ's life—the lesson Milton learnt from God's spirit in his heart—

"They also serve who only stand and wait."

To Christ himself, His Father's business, then, was the development of all His inner self, the maturing for His work. The idea of His mission and the powers for it grew together, and when the time for action came He was ready.

Such times of waiting mark, not uncommonly, our life. Our youth is kept back from the press of labor, or our manhood is forced to pause. It is a period given to us in which to mature ourselves for the work which God will give us to do.

Oh, use it well! Grow in it; do not retrograde. The way we spend it oftentimes in youth is in light indifference or daring bravado; and when the time comes in which the work which God has chosen for us is ready for our energy, we have no instruments to work with, no ideas to expend and express in fruitful labor. The way we spend it oftentimes in manhood is in whining at God's unfairness, as we call it; in complaining regret for past inactivity; and then, when work is again laid before us, we have lost the time during which we ought to have matured ourselves; enfeebled the will by fruitless wailing; chilled the aspirations which kindle, and the faith and hope which sustain, the toiling spirit of a noble workman for the race; we have missed our opportunity, and now we cannot enter on our ministry. Nothing is sadder than the way in which we wilfully spoil our life.

Christian, no time of seeming inactivity is laid upon you by God without a just reason. It is God calling upon you to do His business by ripening in quiet all your powers for some higher sphere of activity which is about to be opened to you. The time is coming when you shall be called again to the front of the battle. Let that solemn thought of dread yet kindling expectancy fill the cup of your life with the inner work of self-development which will make you ready and prepared when your name is called. The eighteen years at Nazreth, what was their result? A few years of action, but of action concentrated, intense, infinite; not one word, not one deed, which did not tell, and which will not tell upon the universe forever.

Eighteen years of silence, and then,—the regeneration of the world accomplished, His Father's business done.

>   Oh, forgive our faithless mind,
>   Raise us from our low estate,
>   Breathe in us the will to find
>   Higher life in small and great.
>
>   Give us watchful eyes and clear,
>   Purgèd from the scales of sense,
>   Seeing still the Master near,
>   And the city far from hence.

TEACH us, O Lord, to submit ourselves both now and ever to Thy will and providence, and to cast all our care on Thee, who never leavest those that love Thee; and grant that we may so seek the kingdom of God and His righteousness, that all good things may be added unto us; through Jesus Christ our Lord. *Amen.*

Sixth Friday.

Surely He hath borne our griefs, and carried our sorrows: He was wounded for our transgressions, He was bruised for our iniquities : the chastisement of our peace was upon Him ; and with His stripes we are healed.

The Lord hath laid on Him the iniquity of us all.

Then delivered he Him therefore unto them to be crucified. And they took Jesus and led Him away. And He, bearing His cross, went forth.

"THEN delivered He Him." Now close the temple, ye sons of Aaron ; the types and shadows with which ye had to do have done their duty, now that the Substance has appeared. Lay aside the band from your foreheads, and the breastplate, ye ministers of the sanctuary ; for know that another now justly adorns Himself with both, and that your priesthood has reached its termination.

The soldiers have made their preparations, the awful sign has appeared, which has since become the standard of the kingdom of Christ and the token of our salvation. During the space of three thousand years it was constantly symbolized to the view of the believing Israelites. It is even reflected in the peculiar manner in which the dying patriarch Jacob, with crossed hands, blessed his grandsons Ephraim and Manassah. It glimmered no less in the wave offerings of the tabernacle and temple, which, as is well known, were wont to be waved so as to make the form of a cross appear. In the wilderness, the sign was elevated to support the brazen serpent, and the spirit of prophecy interwove it in the figurative language of David's Psalms when placing in the mouth of the future Messiah the words, " They pierced My hands and My feet."

Yonder they conduct the Man of Sorrows! One cannot reflect who it is that is thus laden with the accursed tree without feeling one's heart petrified with surprise and astonishment. But it is well for us that He traversed this path. Only observe how the form of the Lamb which taketh away the sins of the world is so clearly expressed in Him. Behold Him, and say if you do not feel as if you heard the ancient words proceed from His silent lips: " Sacrifice and offering Thou didst not desire, a body hast Thou prepared for Me. Lo! I come, I delight to do Thy will, O my God, yea, Thy law is within My heart." Had He shrunk back from this fatal path, His road to suffering would have represented to us that on which, when dying, we should have quitted the world. Instead of soldiers, the emissaries of Satan would have escorted; instead of the accursed tree, the curse of the law itself; instead of fetters, the bands of eternal wrath would have encircled us, and despair have lashed us with its fiery scourge. Now, on the contrary, angels of peace, sent by Eternal Love, will at length bear us on a path of light, illumined by heavenly promises, to Abraham's bosom.

Certainly, it may still be the case that, during our earthly pilgrimage, we are led on similar paths to that on which we see Jesus, our head, proceeding. For the world hates His members, like Himself; and Satan ceases not to desire to have His redeemed, that he may sift them as wheat. But heaven is no longer closed over our path of suffering and disgrace, nor does the black cloud of rejection and the curse obscure it. The sword of God has returned to its scabbard, and peace and hope are the gracious companions who walk by our side. Christ has deprived our fearful path of its horrors, our burdens of their overpowering weight, our disgrace and need of their deadly stings, and placed us in a situation to say, with the royal Psalmist: "Yea, though I walk through the valley of the shadow of death, I will fear no evil: for Thou art with me; Thy rod and Thy staff they comfort me."

Blessed, therefore, be the faith of our Prince of Peace on the cross! Let us not cease to accompany Him daily thereon in the spirit. It will unspeakably sweeten our own painful path; for why does He take this horrible road, but to enable us to traverse ours with heads erect, because we are freed from curse and care? Upon His path He not only carries our sins to the grave, and breaks a passage through all the obstacles which blocked up our access to the Father, but He makes, at the same time, all the bitter waters of the desert sweet, and neither leaves nor forsakes us till He brings us safe to our heavenly home.

> The Cross is heavy in thy human measure,
>   The way too narrow for thy inward pride;
> Thou canst not lay thine intellectual treasure
>   At the low footstool of the Crucified.

SIXTH FRIDAY.

Oh, that my faithless soul one hour only
Would comprehend the Christian's perfect life;
Despised with Jesus—sorrowful and lonely—
Yet calmly looking upward in the strife.

O CHRIST, O Son of God, whom Thy Father delivered up for us all when He accepted Thee as the true Oblation for us, hearken to the prayers of Thy people, save those whom Thou hast purchased, quicken those whom Thou hast freed, suffer not to go into everlasting mourning those whom Thou didst come to redeem, lest they should perish eternally. Thou who didst endure the Cross for us, pierce our hearts with the nails of Thy fear, that here we may obtain remission of our sins, and in the world to come, eternal joy; through Thee whom we believe to have been crucified for all, and who livest with the Father and the Holy Ghost one God, world without end. *Amen.*

Sixth Saturday.

Looking for and hasting unto the coming of the day of God.

Abide in Him; that, when He shall appear, we may have confidence.

Watch ye therefore, for ye know neither the day nor the hour when the Son of Man cometh.

At the time appointed the end shall be.

WE are not yet in our home; not as yet do we reign; things around us still dazzle us; self-pleased thoughts may yet mislead us; we have still, while yet we are in the flesh, to strike closer and closer into the narrow way, closer and closer to cleave to God, more and more to part with all which would keep us from God. And so God often brings things around us to a sudden end, or brings us in our own sight near the end, that so we may see things more as we shall see them in the end. Seasons of sorrow or sickness, or approaching death, have shown persons a whole life in different colors from what it wore before; how what before seemed "grace" was but "nature;" how seeming zeal for God was but natural activity; how love of human praise had robbed men of the praise of God; how what they thought pleasing to God was only pleasing self; how one subtle, self-pleasing sin has cankered a whole life of seeming grace. Wherever, then, we may be, in the course heavenward, morning by morning let us place before ourselves that morning which has no evening; and purpose we to do that, and that only, which we shall wish we had done, when we shall see it in the light of that morning when in the brightness of His presence every plea of self-love which now clouds our eyes shall melt away. Evening by evening set we before us that night "wherein no man can work," and resolve we, by God's grace, to work on the morrow, if we see it, more steadfastly the works of God. "Place daily," says St. Anselm, "place daily before your eyes your end. Think most intently whose those things shall be, what they shall profit you, which shall remain after you. Think whither ye shall go; what ye shall carry with you;

what, sent before by you, ye shall find there. Of a truth, ye shall not carry thither nor find there aught but your own deeds, good or bad. This think ye; these things meditate, by night and by day, in public or in private; this be your converse together, What do we? Why linger we? Near is our last day. How spend we our life? How make we amends to God for our sins? Prepare we, as seeing close to us the day of our calling hence, and so fashion ourselves that we may, without fear, go to judgment, since there we shall receive what we have done in the body, good or bad."

Shrink we not, although, as we bring our works near to the light of that Day, much seeming good be shown to us to be real evil, or full of imperfection. Shrink we not, although our seeming treasure melt away, and wherein we thought ourselves rich we find ourselves poor; shrink we not, although the fire of that Day, while it burns away our dross, scorch us; draw we not back, although by that light we see that we must part with this self-indulgence, or sloth, or quickness of temper, or that cherished way of acting, which has wound close around us self-esteem, or love of the praise of man, or even longing for human sympathy. Rather offer we ourselves, in union with the All-atoning Sacrifice, to love nothing, to prize nothing, to wish for nothing, to fear nothing, to hold nothing, to regret nothing, but what we shall love, prize, wish for, or be glad we had feared, held, regretted, when our Saviour and Judge's voice shall utter those dread words, "It is done." So, baring ourselves more and more of all unpleasing unto Him, shall we, with less sluggish steps, follow Him who emptied Himself of all which was His that He might give us all. Nor, having chosen or wishing to choose the better part, think we that it will be long and wearisome to do without this or that; let not Satan turn or hold us back by telling us we can never hold on so long without this or that; think we it not a weary, dreary future to wait so long for the coming of the Lord. His coming draweth nigh; with each decaying year the tokens thicken of the world's decay, the closing strife, the coming of our God.

> Whilst the careless world is sleeping,
> Blest the servants who are keeping
> Watch, according to His word,
> For the coming of their Lord.

Heard ye not your Master's warning?
He will come before the morning,
Unexpected, undescried;
Watch ye for Him open-eyed.

Teach us so to watch, Lord Jesus
From the sleep of sin release us;
Swift to hear Thee let us be;
Meet to enter in with Thee.

O LORD Jesus Christ, who hast promised to come again in like manner as Thou didst go into heaven; we pray Thee to hasten the time of Thine advent, that sin and death may be overcome, and that we, with all Thy faithful departed, may be perfected in blessedness in that day when Thou makest up Thy jewels; through Thy mercy who art blessed and livest with the Father and the Holy Ghost one God, world without end. *Amen.*

Palm Sunday

And they that went before, and they that followed, cried, saying, Hosanna; Blessed is He that cometh in the name of the Lord.

And He cometh, and findeth them sleeping, and saith unto Peter, Simon, sleepest thou? Couldest not thou watch one hour?

IT was less than five days after the immense popular excitement which drew the multitudes of city and country into a jubilant procession of welcome and honor, with palms and garments strewn in the road, to greet the Prophet of Nazareth, conducting Him to the gates of Jerusalem, that He knelt down on the bare ground in the garden, a lonely sufferer, struggling with a secret agony, in which a sense of utter desertion and desolation was one of the bitterest elements; no sound breaking the silence but His groans.

The spot must have been almost the same; for

the rocky path by which the swelling multitude wound over the mount from Bethany to the temple, and this shady orchard of Gethsemane, were both just east of the city gates. Was there ever, then, in the Bible or in history, a more pathetic illustration of the difference between a piety of mere fashion and feeling on the one hand, and a faith of solid principle, rooted in real convictions, equal to all shocks, surviving all trials and changes, on the other? Here, at the garden, the artificial stimulants have ceased to act; the pageant has passed; the crowd is scattered; the fascination of popularity has waned; and so the very friends and Apostles of the holy Sufferer lose their interest; they sleep with the sleeping world when they ought to watch and pray. How fearful is that *power* of outside show and custom which can outdo the heart's own affection and faith! How fearful is the *weakness* of inward principle which yields up its vigilance and trust when the moment of social excitement has gone by!

The palm-branches, and the slumberers; the shouted hosannas, and the heavy eyes,—we see in them, by contrast, the religion of impulse and the religion of principle.

Sometimes there is an apparent beginning of Christian zeal and Christian action in the exhilarating contagion of social example. It is a time perhaps of unusual manifestations of religious fervor. The air seems to be charged with a kind of spiritual electricity,—an excellent tonic if rightly mixed with the more stable and nutritious elements that sustain vitality. All the frame glows and kindles under it. Many are coming to Confirmation and Communion,—why not I? It looks now as if it would be no very difficult matter to breathe ecstatic breath as daily air; easy enough, while that novel excitement, roused by agitating preaching or extraordinary measures, continues to pull off the garments of reserve or hesitation and strew them in the Lord's way; easy enough to practise jubilee discipline while all the ardent family do it; easy enough to rank with the anxious, and to relate an experience, when a sacred fanaticism stirs a multitude. Why not move with the moving procession? Yes; it is well to move, and to be moved. Only the test is coming,—the trial-night of Gethsemane, —solitude, temptation, watchfulness, unnoticed and unapplauded sacrifices. Be sure here is something more than surface-feeling, set awake by cus tom or animal stimulus; something more than impulse; it is good, honest, sober, considerate, patient *principle*, stayed up by prayer, that alone can *remain* awake and outwatch the stars, and wait through the darkness, and conquer temptation, and do it all for the honor of the suffering and bleeding Master. It is only this that proves that we are really Christians, or that Christ is ours.

The palm-strewing and shouting multitude were not deliberate hypocrites; the pharisees stayed at home and washed their platters. But none the less was the homage vain; and it is no wonder if the Saviour, who saw its emptiness—and how deep was that emptiness!—wept in the midst of it. He foresaw Gethsemane on the eve of the Passover, the slumberers there, the closed eyes, the weak flesh, the denial, the judgment-hall, the cross. And *now*, would we not find the same sorrow on His face if we beheld Him looking on many of our thin and frivolous usages of popular confession and discipleship,—" the form of godliness without the power thereof?"

Yes, there is a dull insensibility to a Benefactor's anguish, there is a sleepy indifference to a Saviour's work, which is nothing less than cruelty. Many of us would rather our enemies should sharpen the spear, or drive thorns into our foreheads, than that our friends should shut their eyes and deny their sympathy to our pain. We give Christ nothing unless we give Him our hearts.

Take away from our prevailing religious observances, even in our more solemn seasons, all that is wholly a deference to decent social standards and conventional Christianity, all that is formal repetition and going with the multitude; empty the sanctuaries of all worshippers who come, not for Christ's sake, but because others come; take down, stone by stone, and timber by timber, all the temples that were built up by vanity, or competition, or a dead compliance with a kind of external law; arrest and extinguish all professedly Christian charities that are carried on by pride, emulation, ostentation, and self-will, with only a feeble mixture of nobler and purer motives; take out of the charity to Christ's poor all that is put there by a sort of holiday benevolence; sift our customs by this fan in the hands of some searching John Baptist or the mightier Judge that comes after him, and we shall see why the Palm-Sunday story is put into the Gospels, and why it stands here with a warning note of examination on the threshold of Holy Week. We there see, perhaps, how unfit we ourselves are to go down into the deep life, sorrow, loneliness, and agony of Gethsemane, to watch and pray there with the awful tortures of the Man of Sorrows, to see the angel from heaven strengthening Him, and to pass thence, faithfully at His side, to the trial, the buffeting, and the mournful Mount of Calvary.

> The rocky path still climbs the glowing steep
>   Of Olivet:
> Though rains of two millenniums wear it deep,
>   Men tread it yet.
>
> These ways were strewed with garments once and palm,
>   Which we tread thus:
> Here, through Thy triumph, on thou passedst calm,—
>   On to Thy Cross.
>
> Man has not changed them in that slumbering land,
>   Nor time effaced:
> Where Thy feet trod to bless, we still may stand,—
>   All can be traced.
>
> Yet we have traces of Thy footsteps far
>   Truer than these;
> Where'er the poor, and tried, and suffering are,
>   Thy steps faith sees.

And now whenever meets Thy lowliest band,
 In praise and prayer,
There is Thy presence, there Thy Holy Hand,
 Thou, Lord, art there!

O GOD of wonderful goodness and power, who by Thy words and works dost command us, though unworthy servants, to hope for true and everlasting blessings in Thee, and from Thee; grant unto us Thy servants such fervent hope in Thee as may rouse us to make our calling and election sure. In Thee, O Lord, have we trusted, let us never be confounded; through the merits of Jesus Christ our Saviour. *Amen.*

Monday in Holy Week.

And seeing a fig-tree afar off having leaves, He came, if haply He might find anything thereon: and when He came to it, He found nothing but leaves; for the time of figs was not yet. And Jesus answered and said unto it, No man eat fruit of thee for ever. And Jesus went into the temple, and began to cast out them that sold and bought in the temple, and overthrew the tables of the money-changers, and the seats of them that sold doves. And he taught, saying unto them, My house shall be called of all nations the house of prayer, but ye have made it a den of thieves.

It is not anywhere expressly announced in the New Testament, but it is a fact strikingly embodied in the very structure of its contents, that while the four Evangelists are so guided by the Spirit which inspires them, that the narrative or assertion of one or two of them is deemed sufficient in authority and fulness for giving us most of the events and discourses in our Saviour's ministry, yet they must all alike pause and dwell in minute detail, and with reverential particularity, on the august incidents which immediately precede, accompany, and follow His last suffering, clustering around the Cross. How impressive is this silent tribute to the transcendent majesty and the supreme efficacy of His Passion above all His words and other acts in the redemption of the world! Because every man's first want is reconciliation, atonement, and forgiveness for sin, every possible mark of historical certainty, and every seal of authenticity, must be set on the recital of that Divine miracle. The story bears the stamp of a fourfold verification. No repetition can be wearisome or superfluous in descriptions so fraught as these are with the intense and personal interest of our own deliverance from death into life. It is therefore wisely appointed by the Church that, from the first day of Holy Week on, we shall read over and over the several records of these four Evangelists, holding before us all the manifold touches and colorings given to the solemn portraiture by the individual witnesses and historians, till every essential feature is engraven on the believing heart, and our souls are steeped in the spirit and power of the scene. And now, as to-day we stand looking toward Calvary, where the one great consummation is reached and finished, in which, whether as Messiah or God-man or Redeemer or the loving and obedient Son, He suffers to give us peace, and bleeds to make us clean, and dies once that we may live forever, so we see the four evangelic witnesses each bringing his own separate evidence and contribution to assure the believer and to glorify the Cross, as in turn they all take their glory from it. "The fulfilment of type and shadow, of the hopes of patriarchs, of the expectations of prophets, yes, and of the dim longings of a whole lost and wicked world, must be declared by the whole evangelistic company; the four streams that go forth to water the earth must here meet in a common channel; the four winds of the Spirit of Life must here be united in one."

We will turn now a moment to the chief occurrences which give a special and individual character to this second day of the great Week.

The evening before—the excitement of the palm procession and the triumphal reception being over—as He was starting on His return to Bethany after this wearisome pageant, "Jesus entered the temple and looked round about upon all things."

The words are few and simple; but the hush of a very deep and awful veneration falls on our minds as we even partially conceive what the thoughts were that must have accompanied that look, what events were impending, and what shadows were gathering. The morning explained this silent inspection of the courts of His Father's house. As once near the beginning, so here at the close of His great work of life, the Son of God cleanses His Father's house, with holy and indignant zeal, of its secular profanations. What does the purifying mean? It means that every true, right work in this world must begin and end with the reverent acknowledgment of God our Father; it means that in every Christian life, of man or woman, youth or child, large and clean and unobstructed place must be made for prayer; it means that business must be marked off from worship with a fully drawn and definite line, not suffered under any pretext or apology to take more than its share of time or thought, or to intrude into the sanctuary, or to do what is just as bad,—hold men out of the sanctuary. And this line is not one that shall prevent the influences of the sanctuary and the power of the Gospel from passing out to hallow all the world and sanctify all work, but one that shall save God's public name and ordinances from being swallowed up and defiled in the extortions of Mammon. It means that neither outwardly, in sordid acts, nor inwardly, in selfish, exclusive, uncharitable dispositions, are we to make our Father's house a house of merchandise. And let us not forget that there is a spiritual and real sense in which the whole world of our life is our Father's house.

And then, as in the whole spirit of our Christian faith, the labors of a practical and merciful righteousness follow close and certainly after the prayers and praises of church or chapel or closet, so here in the example of our Lord's humility: no sooner had He asserted the necessity and sacredness of the ordinances of worship and sacrifice, than "the blind and the lame came to Him in the temple, and He healed them." How long will it be, after our feet bear us out of the temple doors, before some sick relative or neighbor, some blind heart, some lame soul, will require our patient and cheerful ministration, and so put to the proof the worth of these sacrifices of the lips?

It was the same day that, as He was walking toward the city, the demands of that hunger which again makes us see how thoroughly mortal His mortal nature was, directed the attention of His disciples to the fig-tree—which, although the time of figs was not yet, held out, by its unusual flourish of premature and leafy pretension, a promise of refreshment—the mortifying symbol of how many human figures all about us, whose only sign of life is the parade and rattle of their barren profession! Most reasonably is it asked, "Why marvel we that like the watered earth that bringeth not forth herbs meet for the use of man, but beareth only thorns and briers, that emblematic tree was now nigh unto cursing, and that its end was to be burned? The dews of heaven had fallen upon it, the sunlight had fostered it, the sheltering hillside had protected it, all seasonable influences had ministered to it, and all had been utterly in vain; the issue was a barrenness that told not only of frustrated but of perverted influences; gifts from the God of nature received only to issue forth in unprofitable and deceptive produce; not in the fruit of His appointment, but in nothing but unseasonable leaves." Before the day ended, there was to be another tribute,—welcome always to the Shepherd and Saviour of the young, in the music of their spontaneous singing. There were children crying in the temple for Him that purified both its rooms and their breasts,—" Hosanna to the Son of David." It must have been an inspiration from above that touched their lips and their eyes. Jesus called it the perfecting of praise, as David himself prophetically had called it. Their chant must have rested Him, amidst the scowls and gibings of the scribes and pharisees.

This night our Blessed Master comes not to Bethany, but to us. Know ye not that ye are the temple of the Holy Ghost? Is it with sadness that He looks round about upon that hidden sanctuary? What does He see in its open courts—in its hidden chambers? Is it the house of prayer? and of what further sacrilege does it need yet to be purged? and what will the scourge of knotted cords be that must purge it?

The trees, too, are here. The Lord comes to-day to these,—hungering still for our love and our service and our holiness. What more can He do, as the prophet asks, to make them fruit-bearing, that He hath not done? Are there leaves only? and if there is some fruit, is it pinched, bitter, boasted of? Or is it fruit that He will gather and keep?

MONDAY IN HOLY WEEK.

Nothing but leaves; the Spirit grieves
 Over a wasted life ;
Sin committed while conscience slept,
Promises made but never kept,
 Hatred, battle, and strife ;
  Nothing but leaves!

Nothing but leaves ; no garnered sheaves
 Of life's fair, ripened grain ;
Words, idle words, for earnest deeds ;
We sow our seeds,—lo! tares and weeds ;
 We reap with toil and pain
  Nothing but leaves!

O HOLY and merciful Saviour, Thou most worthy Judge Eternal, who as on this day didst curse the fig-tree bearing leaves and not fruit, take away from me all hollow, vain, and false show, and make me plenteously to bring forth the fruit of good works, and of Thee to be plenteously rewarded, through Thy merits, who with the Father and the Holy Ghost livest and reignest ever one God, world without end. *Amen.*

Tuesday in Holy Week.

And in the daytime He was teaching in the temple; and at night He went out, and abode in the mount that is called the Mount of Olives. And all the people came early in the morning to Him in the temple, for to hear Him.

Then Jesus said unto them, Yet a little while is the light with you. Walk while ye have the light, lest darkness come upon you: for he that walketh in darkness knoweth not whither he goeth. While ye have light, believe in the light, that ye may be the children of light. These things spake Jesus, and departed, and did hide Himself from them.

DRAWING nearer to the Mount of Sacrifice, we find it was on the third day of the great Week that Christ said so much in His solemn conversations and parables of the assaults of our spiritual enemies. These powers of darkness, represented in the selfishness, pride, and malice of the influential class at Jerusalem, seeing that their time was short, arrayed this morning all their craft and mustered all their forces. "Is it lawful to give tribute unto Cæsar or not?" Cæsar stood then for all the power of this world,—for the Empire and Rome. "Render unto God the things that are God's." Have you ever taken pains to think how much ground of your heart and your life that covers? What are these "things that are God's?" What share has He; what rights of ownership, creation, preservation; what title, what claims, in your bodily strength, in your time, in your real or personal estate, in your mind and its education, in your tongue and its speech, in your business and its profits, in your social influence and its motives, in your home-happiness and the fruits of it? In your habitual way of estimating these things, and talking about them, do you treat them as His, in any sense,—His so as to be used for Him,—His to be left with you or taken away from you as may be His perfect will,—His to be accounted for to Him? or is it the habit of your mind to regard them all as your own, in some exclusive and self-gratifying way, as if your rights in them would never be invaded,—as if no hand but yours could be laid upon them? Take any one of your most precious possessions; set it before you in the solemnity of your hour of solemn communion with your Maker and Judge; put this question: What are the things of God in relation to this my child and his training for eternal life? What are the things of God in my every-day employment; in my conduct toward my family; in my amusements; in my very dress and manners and food and drink? What are God's claims here? What change would come over my practices and my actions here if I could say, truly, Such is my hunger and thirst after holiness, it is my meat and drink to do the will of God?

In the same day, as He walked the courts of the temple which He had cleansed of its profanations, Jesus saw the rich casting their ostentatious gifts into the treasury, and a poor widow laying all that she had at the feet of Him who gives *us* all that we have. She had found out how to render unto God the things that are God's, not stinting herself to those offerings which cost her nothing. As she drew back her empty hand, and went away to toil for more, what countless riches Christ poured into her everlasting keeping,—" She hath cast in more than they all." New measurements, new standards of value, new reckonings of much and little.

high and low, humble and exalted, strong and weak, the Gospel brings. The first shall be last, and the last first. It was so not then only, but it is so in all temples, it is so in all lands, it is so in every branch of the Church.

> The censer swung by the proud hand of merit
> Fumes with a fire abhorred;
> While faith's two mites, dropped covertly, inherit
> A blessing from the Lord.

Even on earth the eyes of man are not so wholly discolored as not to see this superior spiritual beauty. As with the Mary that we read of in the Gospel yesterday, whose unpretending offering of ointment at Christ's feet was only a waste in the cold calculation of the thrifty bystanders, so a woman's profounder economy of simple affection and trust, making self poor for Jesus' sake, goes out as a perfume through the earth; and wheresoever the Gospel of the Cross is preached, her deed is a part of its story of self-renunciation. As the Holy Weeks come round, do they find us any nearer to the measure of devotion that the Saviour accepted and blessed?

As the same day wears on, some Greeks—proselytes to Judaism—that had come up to Jesus, with the characteristic curiosity of the Greek intellect, hearing the rumors of this new Nazarene Philosopher—as they doubtless esteemed Him—speak words that beautifully utter our deepest need, in spite of all the intellectual culture and refinement and strength in the world,—the cry of sin: "Sir! we would see Jesus!" Beholding in this confession the sign and prophecy of the final victory of His cause, Christ exclaims that the hour is come when the Son of Man should be glorified. But instantly the remembrance of the Cross, which tinges every moment, rises in His mind. Faithful as ever, though it may discourage and repel the questioners, He fearlessly announces that only through the unsightliness of death can His true kingdom unfold itself, and the Tree, whose leaves are for the healing of the nations, fill the earth. "Except a corn of wheat fall into the ground and die, it abideth alone: but if it die, it bringeth forth much fruit. He that loveth His life shall lose it; if any man serve Me, him will My Father honor."

Other momentous acts and words were crowded into this full day; the reply that disarmed the doubts of the Sadducees; the announcement to the shallow scribe of the one great commandment; the rebukes of the pharisees for inconsistent and self-seeking dogmas; and those most penetrating parables, like that of the Ten Virgins, which show us the shortness of the time, the greatness of the work, the blessed bridal welcome of those that enter with burning lamps, and the shutting of the door.

But, before the night falls, there is one august scene more. Many generations before, the prophet Zechariah, foretelling the final coming and judgment, for which the world is still looking, saw the curtain lifted, and wrote thus: "His feet shall stand in that day upon the Mount of Olives, which is before Jerusalem on the east." Now, in most unforeseen coincidence, as the evening shadows gather, the Messiah moves out of the city eastward, and, His feet standing on that very spot of Olivet, He declares to the ages that one solemn prediction which should always keep them in expectation of His reappearing, ending, "Then shall they see the Son of Man coming with power and great glory; and He shall send His angels, and they shall gather together His elect from the four winds, from one end of heaven to the other."

How it comforts our hearts, and brings our Lord very near to our poor human feeling and weakness once more, after these awe-inspiring wonders, to read that at the end of the day, with the same earthly air breathing on His forehead that refreshes our weariness, He walks out with His disciples to the family circle and home, to rest with those that His human affection loves at Bethany.

> Virgins ten, with joyous feet,
> Forth the Bridegroom went to meet;
> Wise with heavenly wisdom, five
> Kept with oil their lamps alive;
> Five, with earth-born folly dim,
> Scorned with oil their lamps to trim.
>
> While the Bridegroom yet delayed,
> Slumber bowed each virgin head;
> Sudden rose the midnight cry,
> "Lo! the Bridegroom draweth nigh!"
> Rose the startled virgin train,
> Trimmed their dying lamps again.
>
> Vainly now for oil ye cry;
> Foolish virgins, hence, and buy.
> Haste the five, but now the door
> Closes on them evermore;
> And a voice, that stuns each heart,
> Cries, I know you not, depart.

FIX, O Lord, my thoughts and my desires upon heaven and heavenly things; teach me to despise the world, to repent me deeply for my sins; give me holy purposes of amendment and Divine strength and assistance to perform faithfully whatsoever I shall intend piously. Enrich my understanding with an eternal treasure of Divine truths, that I may know Thy will, and that Thou workest in us both to will and to do of Thy good pleasure. Teach me to obey all Thy commandments, to believe all Thy revelations, and make me a partaker of all Thy gracious promises, for Jesus Christ's sake. *Amen.*

Wednesday in Holy Week.

And the first day of unleavened bread, when they killed the passover, His disciples said unto Him, Where wilt thou that we go and prepare that Thou mayest eat the passover?

And He sendeth forth two of His disciples, and saith unto them, Go ye into the city, and there shall meet you a man bearing a pitcher of water: follow him, and wheresoever he shall go in, say ye to the good man of the house, The Master saith, Where is the guest-chamber, where I shall eat the passover with My disciples? And he will show you a large upper room furnished and prepared: there make ready for us.

IN the narrative of the Evangelists, there is one sentence that falls on the ear with the startling impression of a double sense. In the preparation for the Passover, Jesus sent forward St. Peter and St. John, in the streets of Jerusalem, to an unknown resident there, with this question, "The Master saith unto thee, Where is the guest-chamber where I shall eat the passover with My disciples?" The walls of that city widen out, as we read, to the width of the world. Peter and John are only the messengers of that Word which has gone out into all the earth. The Passover is the spiritual feast of the Lord's presence and fellowship,—His truth and faith, His hope and charity. And who is the man bearing the pitcher of water, going on some poor commonplace errand, busy with some narrow business, plodding along a routine of daily work which seems to be altogether of the earth, earthy,—little mindful who is at hand, and what a glory waiting at his door? Who is he but you, and you, one and another of these ordinary half-awakened people? Unto thee the Master saith, "Where is the guestchamber where I shall eat the passover with my disciples?" It is a personal question. It is a proposal to the inner life of us all. It is an offer of the one Infinite Divine blessing, for, in receiving the Master, Christ, the Son of Mary and the Son of God, we receive all the real good there is in earth and heaven. And is it not just after this manner that the one great revelation and disclosure is almost always made to us that we can be privileged to welcome and entertain Him, by that keen, real, living sense of which the best name is faith? Is it not apt to be while we are on the way of some familiar duty, in some path that we did not strike out for any great purpose, that the messenger of God meets us,—a sharp Providence abrupt as Peter, or a breath of God's loving spirit gentle as John? So, if now, in the midst of our Christian heritage, some of us find our feeling too dull, our prayers too lifeless, and our sense of things divine too cold, we may be sure we are not to gain the livelier feeling or the awakened zeal by waiting till some rare occasion or great opportunity shall overtake us. It will come when we are in the common lot and about common labors. We are to expect it then, look for it then, make ready for it there. It will come not so much by our going to a new place, a new set of circumstances, or looking out for a propitious season—for these are very apt to prove perverse, and disappoint us after all—as by our opening the eyes and the ears of our hearts, and, when the voice speaks to us, stopping to listen, and, as the prophet says, standing still to see the salvation of God.

"Where is the guest-chamber where I shall eat the passover?" the Master saith. There seems to be in this question just that twofold sound of invitation and authority, offer and command, which is always to be found in the word of the Saviour when He proposes to take up His abode in any of our hearts. He offers to come in if we will suffer Him; for the act must be free. He commands us to suffer Him, because he has a right there; the upper chamber is His; and though faith holds the key to it, we cannot keep Him out without disobedience to Him, and guilt and misery following. This is what our Christian life—part a task and part a delight, part duty and part privilege, part drudging and part festival, part of law and part of grace—must always include, the proportions of the service of obligation and the service of joy constantly varying, according as we have more or less of the Master's own spirit, and live nearer to Him. The man bearing the pitcher of water might have taken this most delicately and condescendingly worded message to him only as a compulsory requirement, and have gone about the labor of opening his house to these strangers as an irksome necessity, or he might hail the notice sent him as only a coveted permission, and so have sprung to seize the honor and the pleasure, as love always answers to the call of love. There is this radical, deep difference between our two kinds of compliance with our Lord's word. It is plain enough with the householder which would be the true hospitality, so with all of us which would be the accepted and loyal service, carrying the affections, the hands, the feet, the lips, the offerings of time and money cheerfully with it, and making the Divine Guest truly at home in the guest-chamber of the heart. " Thou shalt do well," says a very devotional and saintly writer on the Holy Communion, evidently with this same image in his thoughts, " to imitate the example of a poor countryman, who, understanding that the king would visit his house, removed all things that he thought might offend his eyes, did very diligently sweep all his house, and although he could not beautify it according to the worthiness of such a guest, yet did as much as ever he was able to receive him worthily. What, then, wilt thou do to the King of kings, who loveth but to impart His good gifts unto thee? Labor, therefore, in cleansing and decking thyself; hanging the chamber or upper room of thy best devotions with the tapestry of holiness, and welcome Him with love, who out of very love hath said, My delight is to be with the sons of men."

And what it is in you that needs to be put out

of the chamber, before Christ can be worthily received there, it is not for any mortal tongue to tell, but it is not beyond your reach, with the Bible, with secret prayer, with the holy and helpful ordinances of the Church, to know full well.

  He cometh, as He came of old,
   Suddenly to His Father's shrine;
  Into the hearts He died to make
   Meet temples for His grace Divine.

  He cometh, as the Bridegroom comes,
   Unto the feast Himself has spread;
  His flesh and blood the heavenly food
   Wherewith the wedding guests are fed.

  He cometh,—let not one withdraw,
   Nor fear to bring repented sin;
  There's blood to wash, there's bread to feed,
   And Christ himself to enter in.

LORD, I am not worthy that Thou shouldst come under my roof, yet remember that Thou, being Lord of all, didst take upon Thee the form of a servant, and wast the friend of publicans and sinners. Let that humiliation of Thine, I pray Thee, move Thee not to despise me, but do Thou mercifully come unto me, or graciously receive me coming unto Thee. O Blessed Lord, kindle such a holy flame in my heart that it may consume all my sins, that I may never again defile the place which Thou hast chosen for Thy temple. Give me time and space to repent, and give me grace that, as by Thy holy inspiration I do sincerely and steadfastly resolve on an entire reformation, so by Thy merciful guidance I may perform the same. *Amen.*

Maundy-Thursday.

Then cometh Jesus with them unto a place called Gethsemane, and saith unto the disciples, Sit ye here, while I go and pray yonder. And He took with Him Peter and the two sons of Zebedee, and began to be sorrowful and very heavy.

And He said, Abba, Father, all things are possible unto Thee; take away this cup from Me: nevertheless not what I will, but what Thou wilt.

And there appeared an angel unto Him from heaven, strengthening Him. And being in an agony He prayed more earnestly, and His sweat was as it were great drops of blood falling down to the ground.

CHRIST no sooner comes to the garden than He takes His three more confidential disciples, separates Himself from the rest, and begins to be sorrowful and very heavy. The two words in the original text, of which the latter is more emphatic than the former, so as to make a climax, are joined, for the sake of emphasis, to express one thought, together, for the expression of which either word alone would have been too weak. This condition of our Lord the disciples first inferred from His appearance, but soon out of the abundance of His depressed heart His mouth spake. Unable to bear it any longer alone, He said unto them: "My soul"—my very soul, as we should say—"is exceeding sorrowful"—surrounded with sorrow—"even unto death." Stronger expressions than these do not exist in language, and exaggeration is out of the question here. Then, seeing them weary and sleepy, He adds: "Tarry here,"—do not return to the others to sleep; watch with Me! His strength was spent, and for the first time He felt the need of human sympathy. But soon finding even their company burdensome, He tears himself away from them, about a stone's cast, to pray alone. Then He assumes the attitude of deepest distress; He falls "on His face" and pours out His soul. Submission He finds in His heart while praying, but relief He finds none. Distressed, He returns to His disciples, and "findeth them asleep." And He saith unto Peter: "What!"—you have made such professions of attachment to Me, you wanted to die for Me—" could you not watch with Me one hour?" Alas! He pleads for one hour's sympathy and assistance from His weak and drowsy followers. Oh, how destitute must He have felt himself! He goes the second time to pray alone, and finds no relief; He returns the second time to His disciples, and finds no sympathy. Human relief fails; God remains His last hope. Moving away once more, He prostrates himself again,—and now the most awful struggle for life begins. And being in an agony, He prayed more earnestly; and in the cool night season, while prostrated on the damp ground, the sweat of anguish breaks out over His whole body and is as it were great drops of blood falling down to the ground. "And there appeared an angel unto Him from heaven, strengthening Him."

Such, then, was His frame of mind that no ordinary means did suffice to relieve Him; an angel, with an express message and peculiar assurances, must be sent. High and distinguished honor, indeed, to be the bearer of this errand,—an errand before unheard of in heaven! But can you think of anything more fit to impress us with ideas of the most awful—I had almost said unnatural—distress than the need of a messenger from heaven to comfort and strengthen Jesus the Son of God, lest His distress should crush Him?

No doubt it was intended by a holy Providence, and was one of the burdens which Christ had to bear for us, that He suffered destitute of all human consolation. It does seem as though the disciples had been providentially given up to the most stupefying influence of this body of clay to disable them to afford relief to their Master when the unmingled cup of suffering was to be drunk to the bottom.

Jesus our Saviour, in this destitute and needy condition, is an object of the deepest interest and of liveliest gratitude to those who know the secret ways of God with His children. They know every particular sacrifice and deprivation of Christ is like a sown seed, from which rich and waving harvests of spiritual consolation are continually springing up to the dear little flock of His pasture. Not a prayer, not a sigh, not a tear of His, but it procures for them some heavenly treat; and His fastings and deprivations, His watchfulness, weariness, and exposures, are richly decking their spiritual table, and draw the curtain of heavenly peace around the defenceless pillows of their rest. And when, in the depth of anguish, they feel the soothing influences of Christian tenderness and sympathy, and are upheld by the wrestling intercessions of their beloved in Christ Jesus,—when they are carried safely through the trying hour of darkness and distress by the faithful prayers of their watchful friends, poured forth in their hearing at the throne of Grace,—ah! then they remember with sweet and humble gratitude the forsaken Jesus in the garden, and a connection between their spiritual riches and comforts and His destitution becomes clear all at once to their souls, of which they had no conception, perhaps, while in health of body and in the cheerful vigor of heart and mind. They rejoice then exceedingly, with a joy full of glory, that ever He did procure such sweet comforts for their distressed souls; and they are prepared to give Him everlasting thanks for every tear He dropped upon the accursed ground of this world. Yet they are careful, too, to learn the important lesson of Him, when lawful earthly consolations and sympathies fail, to go a little farther, and, where no man can see them, or overhear their prayer, to fall on their faces, and, with naked and unalloyed faith and trust in God, to lean upon His almighty arm alone, and to throw themselves with their burden down at His feet, there to live, or there to die.

Gloomy garden, on thy beds,
　　Wash'd by Kedron's water-pool,
Grow most rank and bitter weeds,—
　　Think on these my soul, my soul!
Wouldst thou sin's dominion see?
Call to mind Gethsemane.

Sins against a holy God;
　　Sins against His righteous laws;
Sins against His love, His blood;
　　Sins against His name and cause;
Sins immense as is the sea:
Hide me, O Gethsemane!

O LORD Jesus Christ, who in the sorrow of Thy soul didst fall down upon Thy face in prayer, give us grace that we likewise in all our sorrows may betake ourselves with humble and earnest prayer to our heavenly Father for aid and comfort and relief. Hear us, O Saviour Jesus Christ, for Thy name's sake, who livest with the Father and the Holy Ghost one God, world without end. *Amen.*

Good-Friday.

And when they were come to the place, which is called Calvary, there they crucified Him, and the malefactors, one on the right hand, and the other on the left.

And when Jesus had cried with a loud voice, He said, Father, into Thy hands I commend My spirit: and having said thus, He gave up the ghost.

Now when the centurion, and they that were with him watching Jesus, saw the earthquake, and those things that were done, they feared greatly, saying, Truly this was the Son of God.

Greater love hath no man than this, that a man lay down his life for his friends.

WE draw near to the Mount of Sacrifice. We stand, nay, we kneel, at the foot of the Cross. We come there now, not because it is the custom of a fast, but because we are driven thither by the burden of our human hearts,—our need of reconciliation by suffering.

Look closely at this want, for it is that vital spot

in all humanity where sorrow is most keen, and where relief is most joyful. The sure result of evil is pain; of persistent sin is death. Hence the voluntary surrender to pain, pain even unto the body's death, is felt, and has been ever felt, to be the natural expression of a penitent soul. It is propitiation: not because God takes pleasure in His children's suffering, but because that is the soul's fitting tribute to the just majesty of goodness and the holy authority of Right. Government without penalty is gone, and all its blessed protections are dissolved. Hence the honest heart cries out in its shame and fear: "Let me suffer for my sin." Suffering for it there must be somewhere; transgression is a costly business; so it must always be and always look; right must stand at any rate; law must be sacred, or all is gone; and since nothing is so dear as life, and blood is the element of life, life itself must be surrendered, and "without the shedding of blood is no remission."

Take the next step. Just because this life is so dear, He who loves us infinitely, and to whom it is dearer than to us, will be willing to lay down for us His own. He will not even wait for our consent; but in the abundance of that unspeakable compassion, in the irresistible freedom of that goodness, He will do it beforehand,—only asking of us that we will believe He has done it, and, accepting our pardon, be drawn by that faith into the same self-sacrificing spirit. Herein is love indeed. Suffering for our peace! Sacrifice, not that our service may profit and pay Him, but that our transgression of a Perfect Law may be pardoned, and the noble life of disinterested goodness may be begotten in ourselves. Before, we had seen God as Creator, Providence, Ruler, and all the motives to obedience furnished by those characters had been offered, and had failed. His servants, the prophets, had come, and come often in vain. But now we see Him in the new, more wondrous, and more gracious character of Sacrifice. The last proof of tenderness is given. "Is not the mystic yearning of love expressed in words most purely thus: 'Let Me suffer for him?'" We want to feel that our God of infinite love feels that. Calvary is the full answer to that want. In the person of the Son He so comes down among us, and into us, as to suffer for us. We have a High Priest that can be touched with the feeling of our infirmities,—nay, takes those infirmities upon Him, bears our sicknesses, is bruised for our iniquities, is delivered for our offences, dies that we may live. All the priestly offices are fulfilled. "Herein is love; not that we loved God, but that God loved us, and sent His Son to be the propitiation for our sins." The atonement by Christ becomes the inmost and grandest power of the world. It is the one peculiar, characteristic, crowning, glorious truth of the Gospel.

And then if you turn from what it does *for* us, as a redemption, to what it does *within* us, as an inspiration, the fruit of it is not less Divine. For it appeals directly to what is noblest, most generous, most disinterested, in all the brave affections and aspirations of humanity. It rises up in harmony with, and surmounts with its grandeur, all the heroic and martyr sacrifices of mankind. Mechanical and mercantile conceptions of salvation vanish before it. Right becomes more venerable; love, more lovely; charity, more beautiful. It was of charity that the Saviour suffered. His Cross teaches us, not that each one is to be looking out for a selfish salvation, but that self is to be forgotten in hearty consecration to Him, and in free service to our brethren. It carries us clear of the belittling notions of escaping hell as a punishment or earning heaven as a reward. It makes the lofty sentiment of gratitude the mainspring of piety; faith, the pure inspiration of righteousness; love, the sacred secret of beneficence. We learn from the Redeemer, who gave Himself for us, to give ourselves for one another. We take up that Cross which signifies an atoning sacrifice, a voluntary, vicarious humiliation, a making of no reputation and becoming poor, a taking of the form of a servant, and being made an offering for sin for others' sake. Henceforth we abhor sin for itself, for our brethren's sake, for Christ's sake, and not merely for its penal consequences. We love goodness, and are loyal to it for itself; not merely for its wages. We not only "admire philanthropy," but we "love men," as those for whom Christ has been willing to die. We cease longing for rest, and begin to have joy in God, in the "spirit of liberty," and in the eternal life begun.

This is what is meant by Christ our Priest. This is that profound, penitential, sorrowing, unutterable want in human souls which the Redeemer meets, and which, because He meets it, makes the heart that is thus consciously set at liberty leap with gratitude and gladness to join the praises which give blessing and honor and glory to Christ. It will not be for any of us to say there is no need of a blessing so deep and a joy so great. You may say you have not yet felt the need of it; and that —O pity of God!—may be mournfully true. But close by you is some heart which feels that beside this want and its bitterness all the common griefs of mortality are trifles of the air: the want of reconciliation with the Father in heaven; the want of an assured forgiveness; the want of Christ and Him crucified. Where that is once stirred and alive—and the first object of the New Testament is to stir it and make it alive, because that is the only way to peace and power—there you find a heart that only one word of earth or heaven can reach. You may tell it that its sorrow is all needless and irrational, that all we have to do in this world is "to do right," or as near it as we can; but it will only look back upon you with speechless wonder. Do right? What if, with the strongest of apostles, I do not "find how" to do right? What if the right seems to me too high and holy a thing, and too far off, that I should do it of myself? What if, all my life long, by doing or leaving undone, I have come all too terribly short even of the right I knew? Then let me have, what the blessed, merciful Gospel gives me, a Redeemer! Let me rest my heart upon the Cross! Take not away my Lord!

> I thirst, Thou wounded Lamb of God,
> To wash me in Thy cleansing blood,
> To dwell within Thy wounds; then pain
> Is sweet, and life or death is gain.
>
> How blest are they who still abide
> Close shelter'd in Thy bleeding side!
> Who life and strength from Thee derive,
> And by Thee move, and in Thee live!
>
> What are our works but sin and death,
> Till Thou Thy quick'ning spirit breathe!
> Thou giv'st the power Thy grace to move,—
> O wondrous grace! O boundless love!
>
> Ah, Lord! enlarge our scanty thought,
> To know the wonders Thou hast wrought!
> Unloose our stammering tongues, to tell
> Thy love, immense, unsearchable!

O FATHER of mercies, whose blessed Son was on this day crucified for us, the just for the unjust, to bring us to Thee, give us grace we beseech Thee to look in faith upon that Cross, and to crucify ourselves upon it to every sinful desire and unchristian temper. May we learn, in humble devotion to our Master's service, to take up our cross and deny ourselves, that we may follow Him. And grant that looking to His Passion we may be changed to His image as by the Spirit of the Lord, that all carnal affections may die in us, and that all things belonging to the Spirit may live and grow in us, so that we, being buried with Christ in His death, may crucify the old man and utterly abolish the whole body of sin; through the same our Lord and Saviour Jesus Christ. *Amen.*

Easter-Even.

So they went, and made the sepulchre sure, sealing the stone, and setting a watch.

And the women also, which came with Him from Galilee, followed after, and beheld the sepulchre, and how his body was laid.

And they returned, and prepared spices and ointments; and rested the Sabbath day according to the commandment.

THROUGH the silence that falls, the night after the crucifixion, on the city of Jerusalem, and through the shadows that gather about the slopes of the Mount of Olives eastward and in the valley of Kedron between, we can see two groups of watchers before the sepulchre of Jesus. The contrast in their characters, purposes, and feelings, as toward the blessed and royal Figure that sleeps within, furnishes a practical theme for our contemplation this Easter-Even.

The chief priests and pharisees had obtained an order from the Roman procurator, Pilate, for a guard of Roman soldiers; and "they went and made the sepulchre sure, sealing the stone and setting a watch." The object was not to protect the place where the lifeless body of the Best Friend of all men, the greatest of all hearts that ever beat on earth, was lying, but to secure and vindicate their murder. Oh, what a stupendous fiction and phantom of their own deluded brain it was that they were setting these armed soldiers to keep! They feared that the disciples would come to steal the blessed body away! The scheme was just what the ingenuity of the intellect is apt to devise where faith is shut out. The arm of the mightiest military empire on earth was in full play, but it was weaker than a straw. The real keepers of the tomb were angels from the right-hand of another throne. But the stone was sealed, and the guards paced to and fro in the Paschal moonlight, and did their best.

Another part of the narrative shows us a different group,—" And there was Mary Magdalene and the other Mary, sitting over against the sepulchre." Here were vigils of another kind. For what were these waiting and watching? Only for some further opportunity of service; only to testify with further offices of tenderness and love their devotion to Him who had healed, comforted, and saved them. They could lean no longer upon the living arm of the Beloved One. But they could anoint Him, and once more let their tears fall on His feet. They waited till the Sabbath should be past for this; waited obediently; there was no restless running to and fro in the weakness of unbelief; no agitation; no loud grief. They sat still; they watched the eastern sky to catch the first pencil of the dawn toward Hebron; their look turned to and fro, silently, between the tomb and the heavens. "Weeping may endure for a night, but joy cometh in the morning." How clear and full their expectation was that this Third Day would bring back life to the dead, by some miracle greater than any they had seen done by Him, we are not told and cannot know. This we know, that the motive of their watching was a trusting, clinging, reverential, holy love.

The two groups bring strikingly to mind the two clauses of a sentence at the conclusion of the Canticles,—"Love is strong as death; jealousy is cruel as the grave;" the one outlasts and outwatches death, the other is cruel even over the grave. We can hardly help finding an application here for the adjoining words of the same Bible-song: "Thou that dwellest in the gardens, set me as a seal upon thine heart, as a seal upon thine arm. Make haste, my beloved, be thou like to a young hart upon the mountains of spices. Many waters cannot quench love, neither can the floods drown it." May we not say, then, there are two kinds of watching set before us, with very different motives and feelings lying under them and prompting them? One will be the watching of self-will, pride, or formality—Roman self-will, pharisaic pride, the scribe's formality—all of one selfish, faithless spirit. So we watch and so we work when, under the show of protecting the right, we are secretly contriving for and indulging ourselves. So we watch when we let the world become our tyrant, and we are its mercenaries doing its bidding, pacing to and fro on an unhallowed round of heartless frivolities, or surrendering to it the time, strength, zeal, which we know belong to Him who died for us and rose again. So we watch when we are in our hearts wishing the vigil were over, or are glad to escape from the hour and place of prayer, when we tire of the Church's service, or of the Lenten restriction, or of the Sabbatic commandment, or of the homely work that must be done for the least of the Lord's children if it is to be done for Him.

But we would rather on this Easter Even join ourselves to the other company of watchers, sitting over against the sepulchre, looking for the first occasion to do some service more for their Master, " as they that watch for the morning ; " counting it a part of our faith in Christ to try to be like Christ. There are sacrifices of luxury, appearance, or comfort, which are to our Saviour's honor what the ointments of spices were to his body in the sepulchre. We have seen in these past weeks how His body is laid; to how sad an extent His Church lies dead, and how much it needs the inbreathing of a new spirit, or rather the restoration of the original life, that it may go more swiftly and steadily on, conquering the sin and sorrow, cruelty and misery that are in the world This is the way for us, who would honor Christ among men, to watch for Him. Here is a resurrection for which we can make ready. The least of us can bring something every day. Like Joseph of Arimathea, the rich man may do much. Like the widow in the temple, the poor may cast in what they have, and take the wealth of His love who loveth a cheerful giver. Like the women of the Resurrection morning we can, in supplications and intercessions and communions, hold Jesus by the feet and worship Him. And we who mourn continually for some that have departed hence in God's faith and fear, because this was not their Rest, can remember and praise Him, that those who sleep in Jesus God will bring through Paradise into glory, with Him who is the first-fruits of them that sleep. They will be Christ's at His coming.

    Not first the glad and then the sorrowful,—
        But first the sorrowful, and then the glad;
    Tears for a day,—for earth of tears is full,
        Then we forget that we were ever sad.

    Not first the bright, and after that the dark,—
        But first the dark, and after that the bright;
    First the thick cloud, and then the rainbow's arc,
        First the dark grave, then Resurrection light.

    'Tis first the night—stern night of storm and war—
        Long nights of heavy clouds and veilèd skies;
    Then the far sparkle of the Morning-Star,
        That bids the saints awake, and dawn arise.

O LORD Jesus Christ, who by Thy death didst take away the sting of death; grant unto us Thy servants so to follow in faith where Thou hast led the way, that we may at length fall asleep peacefully in Thee, and awaking up after Thy likeness, may be satisfied with it; through Thy mercy who livest with the Father and the Holy Ghost one God, world without end. *Amen.*

THE END.

www.ingramcontent.com/pod-product-compliance
Lightning Source LLC
Chambersburg PA
CBHW021727220426
43662CB00008B/738